BOOKSTORE
PLANNING
AND DESIGN

KEN WHITE, ISP

BOOKSTORE PLANNING AND DESIGN

McGRAW-HILL BOOK COMPANY

New York   St. Louis   San Francisco   Auckland   Bogotá   Singapore
Johannesburg   London   Madrid   Mexico   Montreal   New Delhi
Panama   São Paulo   Hamburg   Sydney   Tokyo   Paris   Toronto

Library of Congress Cataloging in Publication Data
White, Ken.

   Bookstore planning and design.

   1. Book industries and trade—Management.
2. Booksellers and bookselling—Management.
3. Mercantile buildings—Design and construction.
4. College stores.   I. Title.
Z278.W47   070.5′068   81-18658
                                   AACR2

ISBN 0-07-069851-1

1 2 3 4 5 6 7 8 9 0   HDHD   8 9 8 7 6 5 4 3 2 1

The editors for this book were Joan Zseleczky and Carolyn Nagy, the
designer was Elliot Epstein, and the production supervisor was
Thomas G. Kowalczyk. It was set in Garamond by University
Graphics, Inc.

Printed and bound by Halliday Lithograph, Inc.

Dedicated to my wife Adele and the many clients who gave me the opportunity to plan and design so many wonderful projects.

CONTENTS

PREFACE

THE PLANNING, design, and building of a soul-satisfying and successful bookstore requires the coordination of a range of design, architectural, mechanical, and merchandising components to ensure that all elements work together. The role of the bookstore planner is to blend these elements, set forth realistic budgets, and see that both esthetics and functional planning goals are achieved.

This is the first book to be written on the subject. It is intended to be a highly practical one. Its purpose is to provide an overall look at the coordination of all these components primarily for the benefit of the bookseller, administrator, and retail executive who may not have a planning, design, or architectural background. It is also intended for the designer or architect who may have no experience with book merchandising. The book makes no attempt to convert the reader into either a book merchandiser or bookstore design expert. It does broadly discuss the many basic principles and problems encountered in locating, planning, designing, building, expanding, and opening all types of commercial and college bookstores. The reader will learn in Part One how planning, design, architecture, construction, and merchandising of a book department or bookstore are coordinated. Part Two presents a selected group of 23 of the most prestigious and diversified general and specialized trade and college bookstores. Profuse illustrations are given in the portfolio, with numerous plans, drawings, and photographs being published here for the first time.

The difference between small and large bookstores is a matter of scale. The principles dictating planning and design for independent, general, specialized, or college bookstores, chain bookstores, department stores, and discount or mass merchandisers are the same. Only the size, type, and cost vary. The size and type of operation depend on the merchandising concept set by the owners, managers, or administrators, sometimes assisted by outside professional store planning consultants. All final decisions, however, rest with the person designated by the owner to be responsible for seeing that the bookstore is properly planned, built, and opened on time. To that person, this book will be essential.

The owner, manager, or administrator of a bookstore which is being planned must determine whether the consultants, designers, or architects are on target or have "gone overboard" and run project costs sky-high, thus jeopardizing the capital investment. The owner or manager must guard against both letting the merchandising staff take away vital support areas and letting the store operating people commandeer excessive space for maintenance and mechanical facilities. A balance must be maintained.

It is more than likely that the executive ultimately responsible for the project came to that position from other areas of business or book retailing and is not an expert in design, architecture, or construction. Therefore, *Bookstore Planning and Design* is designed to help mesh this person's experience with that of professional bookstore planning and design.

Unless the design or architectural firm called in for professional assistance is experienced with bookstore merchandising and planning, it may not be as effective as with the design of other projects. Bookstore planning *is* an entity unto itself. Retail bookselling principles and criteria discussed in detail in this book will be of value to the designer, architect, or engineer in his or her first encounter with bookshops or college stores.

Only a small percentage of the publishing community has the time or the opportunity to visit as many bookstores as they would like. Publishers and booksellers seldom have the opportunity to look behind the scenes and grasp the full impact of the layout supporting the merchandising concept of the stores, or to learn why certain planning decisions were made. Numerous publishers regularly strive to be of greater assistance to booksellers. Yet, as this book points out, while many of these activities are well meaning, few publishers actually provide the specific kind of creative support stores really need and can use. To those colleagues in the "other half" of the publisher/bookseller partnership, this book will be a revelation.

At some point, the business, marketing, or retailing students of today will be tomorrow's managers, owners, or administrators. It will be necessary for them to be familiar with the techniques of integrating book merchandising with physical planning, design, and construction. The chapters that follow are designed to give just that kind of insight. *Bookstore Planning and Design* will be of value for years to come to the serious student of bookstore retailing.

Descriptions of the basic principles of programming, conceptualizing the idea, and planning apply to almost every type of retail establishment and will be invaluable to students of retailing and bookselling in particular. Finally, the book will be useful to hundreds of small independent booksellers who build their own stores, or who depend on carpenters, contractors, and store fixture manufacturers to build and open, remodel, or expand existing bookstores. These individuals and groups are seldom versed in book merchandising, or may not show much regard for the basic principles of bookstore planning. A high 49 percent of all new bookstores opened are unprofitable. Used as a planning reference, this book could be an aid to help remedy that distressing situation. An innovation in this book is a group of schedules and checklists where a step-by-step approach or summary of vital actions will assist the user in the activity to which it refers.

The Glossary of Bookstore Planning and Design Terms is the first of its type. It is included in the belief that it will be useful and perhaps interesting for the newcomer and veteran booksellers alike when dealing with planning and construction projects.

The numbers interspersed throughout the text refer to the accompanying illustrations of bookstores. There is a comprehensive subject index.

A planning book relating to bookstore design, planning, and construction, is long overdue. The author of this book makes claim neither for originality nor for genius, but hopes that others will come along to fill in the gaps and expand the body of knowledge.

In a first book on any subject, certain matters have to be neglected. I have chosen to concentrate this volume on the work of Ken White Associates, and have not sought to give equal geographic representation to bookstores but have used ones which seemed to be the most appropriate for the story told.

I have many people to thank for their assistance in enabling me to complete this first book, perhaps because the subject is a relatively untouched one and their interest is as great as my own. And my thanks, with great feeling, go to those people who did more than their jobs keeping the office running while I was doing this job.

The clients with whom I have worked were both my educators and benefactors. To them I owe my greatest debt.

I owe other debts as well: to Floyd Hall for giving me the opportunity to plan B. Dalton's 666 Fifth Avenue flagship store; and Dick Fontaine, Jack Ford, and Bob Crabb, whose support and assistance were invaluable; to John Pope, Dave Nelson, and Bobbie Kroman, who made it work.

A final debt is owed to several people who, over the years, helped me form my own sense of what bookselling is all about: Elliot Leonard, Russell Reynolds, G. Royce Smith, the late Sam Hanna, Arthur West, H. Neil McKnight, Lennie Riggio, Al Zavelle, Harlan Davidson, Jim Duffy, Bill Turk, Ray Verrey, and Dave Wellons.

In spite of generally increased book buying and the large volume of bookstore building, we have only begun to meet the need for all kinds of bookstores, including those discussed here. Moreover, I am convinced that bookstore design will become better understood as competition increases.

If this volume helps bring about such an understanding and serves as an aid to booksellers, administrators, architects, publishers, and students of retailing, then it shall have served its purpose.

Ken White
Westwood, New Jersey

ABOUT THE AUTHOR

Ken White, President of Ken White Associates, Inc., a consulting firm specializing in bookstore design, has had more than 30 years' experience and has designed more than 1000 bookstores of all types. A lecturer on bookstore planning and design in the United States and Canada, he has written numerous articles in trade and technical journals. Past President of the Institute of Store Planners, he has also been a designer and consultant to several national trade associations.

BOOKSTORE
PLANNING
AND DESIGN

PART ONE
INTRODUCTION

THE FIRST PURPOSE of Part One is to develop in the reader an awareness of the many activities involved in locating, conceptualizing, planning, building or modernizing, and opening a new bookstore. Part One first defines types of bookstores, the nature of their locations, and types of buildings built for academic bookstores.

The second purpose of Part One is to establish for the reader an awareness of the importance of developing a bookstore planning program, and the roles of the store planner, architect, and, for larger projects, the planning team.

The third major purpose is to examine in depth techniques employed to conceptualize design ideas that lead to preliminary planning. Four chapters are devoted to imparting some understanding of the elements of bookstore design. Chapter 10 explains the technique of getting it all together, and takes us through the preparation of the final project construction plans to the new bookstore opening. Part One is descriptive and attempts to convey an understanding of why successful small and large, private, chain, and institutional retail bookstores follow these planning sequences.

FIRST THINGS FIRST: THE NATURE OF BOOKSTORE PLANNING

I T HAS BEEN SAID, and not necessarily in banter, that bookselling always assures risk and occasionally offers reward. The importance of bookselling is evident from virtually any perspective. Approximately 10,000 bookstores sell books in one form, location, and style in the United States, with over 750 of them in New York City alone. About 1,000 of these bookstores open with the hope and anticipation of success each year. Few are professionally planned.

The relative ease with which it is possible to enter bookselling makes it an appealing way to be independent and to become one's own employer. This probably accounts for the diversity of size, type, ambiance, and appeal of so many bookstores. The importance of bookselling is reinforced because it is one of the most visible of a declining number of opportunities available for the investment of modest sums of individual private capital.

It has also been said that bookselling provides an opportunity for every individual to take at least one bath in a business venture. A great many "baths" have been taken; the number of bookstore failures in the business is very high, according to the American Booksellers Association (ABA). However, better planning could have minimized the number of these failures.

Bookstore planning is fascinating, mostly because bookselling is in a state of constant change; it presents a continuous parade of new titles, products, merchandise, and innovations and new methods of merchandising those items. Bookstore planning and design principles apply to all types of bookstores, small and large; only the scale is different.

TYPES OF RETAIL BOOKSTORES

Classification of retail bookstores according to the book categories and merchandise they carry has produced two distinct types of retail bookstores. Depending on the selection offered, different types of bookstores may be labeled as "general" or "specialty" bookstores. They may differ widely in terms of the completeness of stock they carry. This "completeness" may, in addition, refer to either *assortment* or *variety*.

The term *assortment* means a wide range of choices within a particular book category or generic class of merchandise. A sports book department—a department

Here the design concept is to surround the shopper with books in beams, on tables, and on walls up to the ceiling, so attention is concentrated on the display of books.

B. Dalton, 666 Fifth Avenue, N.Y.C.
(Photo: Bill Mitchell)

that displays and stocks only sports books—is strong in assortments. Similarly, a stationery supply department, with hundreds of wirebound notebooks and stationery supply items and little more, is a retail department featuring stationery supply assortments.

Variety suggests generically different types of books and merchandise, which booksellers call "sidelines." Sidelines include gifts, candy, greeting cards, soft goods, etc. Therefore, a bookstore which offers a great variety is said to be "general."

When a bookstore offers great assortments of one type of merchandise, it is usually a "specialty" bookstore. It literally specializes in a particular field of interest and concentrates on storing and selling a limited number of book categories and classes of merchandise. Ranging from art to zoology, specialty bookstores are identified by the principal category of books they offer for sale.

Because of their broad appeal, general bookstores should be thoughtfully planned and tastefully designed. Certainly, the ambiance of specialty bookstores should be atmospheric and closely relate to the "specialty of the house" concept.

College Bookstores

Most college bookstores are distinguished from commercial trade bookstores in their purpose, book list and merchandise, size, and location. With the exception of medical bookstores and a small number of specialized art and technical stores, the majority of institutionally owned and operated college bookstores are general in nature. Many college stores, of course, have highly specialized and scholarly book departments.

The primary purpose of college bookstores is to have on hand course-related books and supplies available to students and faculty. College bookstores are an adjunct to the educational process. Academic book and merchandise offerings vary from campus to campus, ranging from minimal Spartan shops to some of the largest retail trade and textbook outlets in the country. The majority of college bookstores are small. The distinction between these college bookstores is usually made in terms of (1) their size in square feet of area, (2) the number of students enrolled at the campus, (3) the nature of the academic courses offered, and (4) the nature of nonbook merchandise sold in the bookstore.

Privately owned and cooperative bookstores may also be known as college bookstores. They are so named because of the diverse lines of books and merchandise offered and the specialized skills they have developed and brought to the academic institution they serve.

The few college stores whose sites have been located professionally are outstanding, but this is the exception rather than the rule. Most are in poor locations, tucked away in basements, or otherwise out of sight from the main flow of traffic.

In summary, the terms "general," "specialty," and "college bookstore" refer, at least in part, to the nature of the book categories and merchandise offered.

Retail Chains

A retail bookstore operation is referred to as a chain when it is comprised of more than one bookstore selling the same or similar categories of books and merchandise. Each store has a similar architectural design and graphic motifs, and the operation features centralized buying.

National and regional retail bookstore chains realize their greatest potential in the sale of basic books and staple merchandise. Bestselling books or merchandise for which there is no great variation of customer preference from city to city are the kinds of things that chains do well with. However, titles by regional and local authors are often selected by the chain's resident bookstore manager and centrally purchased through the main office. Thus, a chain bookstore has smaller, differing office space requirements than a general trade bookstore of equal square footage.

Entrance, Harvard Coop, Graduate School of **Business** (*Photo: Phokion Kadas; architect, Kubitz & Pepi*)

Discount, Sale Book Annex, Remainder, and Used Bookstores

Discount bookstores are still another classification for retail bookstores which emphasize low prices and compete aggressively in terms of their prices. However, in the universe of retail bookstores there are only a few booksellers who distinguish themselves as principally concerned with low prices.

In recent years the term *sale book annex* has come on the bookselling scene. Television, newspaper, and radio advertising are heavily employed. These bookstores feature current hardcover titles at discounts (fiction at a 35 percent discount), current mass market and trade paperbacks (at a 20 percent discount), discount classical records, and so forth. These bookstores attract droves of customers and capitalize on this traffic to sell more books and merchandise by regularly featuring *remainder* and hurt books, and used and recycled library books, which can be sold at very low prices and produce a high return.

The size, shape, and variety of important bookstores entirely devoted to selling *used books* is extensive. It is in these stores that customers have their choice of nearly new releases, out-of-print books, and used books at substantial discounts. Chances are, if a customer is looking for a used copy, it can be found in one of these shops. These bookstores do not provide significant in-store services.

When designing a discount, sale book annex, remainder, or used bookstore, the store planner's principal task is to provide imaginative, functional layout arrangements, background color, and graphics. Store fixtures and appointments in the discount bookstore are likely to be scant.

BOOKSTORE LOCATIONS

Since the dawn of history, merchants have tended to cluster together in groups of competing and complementary sellers. Today, "clusters" are as much an institution in bookselling as in general retailing. At present, the most notable cluster of booksellers is on Fifth Avenue between 48th and 58th Streets. It is the most important bookselling row in America! The four principal types of clusters are the central business district (CBD), regional shopping centers, community shopping centers, and neighborhood shopping centers.

The Central Business District

Characteristically, the central business district (CBD) of a city is where the city's main streets converge. The most common retail stores found in the CBD are department stores, specialty apparel shops, restaurants, home furnishing shops, and bookstores. These locations are difficult to obtain; however, as leases on restaurants and mens' and womens' apparel shops come up for renewal, a few occasionally terminate and opportunities open up for booksellers to move into exceptional retail locations.

Most general and nearly all specialty bookstores are situated in CBD locations in major cities. A surprising number of bookstores are hidden in old houses, basements, walkups, and multistoried office buildings; they are tucked into Gothic university buildings, merchandise marts, and the chrome and glass towers of commercial buildings. Many antiquarian booksellers, located in shops, offices, lofts, and private residences, buy, sell, and trade rare and hard-to-find books and manuscripts with each other and their clients by appointment only. Enclosed climate-controlled shopping malls are a reality in a number of CBD situations, most notable of which are Ghiradelli Square, San Francisco; Citicorp, New York City; Watertower Plaza, Chicago; and Omni Center, Atlanta.

The Regional Shopping Center

The suburban cluster development that has been the most impressive, although it is by no means the most numerous, is the regional shopping center. This largest of

Exterior, New Canaan Bookshop *(Photo: Ken White).*

Exterior, Rizzoli International Bookstore of Atlanta, Omni Center *(Photo: Ken White; architect, Fillipo Perego, Milan, Italy)*

all shopping centers is defined as a group of commercial establishments planned, developed, owned, and managed as a unit, with off-street parking provided on the property (in direct ratio to the building area). Regional centers range in area from 400,000 square feet up to 1,000,000 square feet, or more. Regional shopping centers are often laid out as pedestrian *climate controlled enclosed malls* using a CBD pattern of stores on each side of a straight thoroughfare, turning or branching in an X, T, or L from it.

This center requires a market of 100,000 to 1,000,000 persons with a buying power of $50,000,000 to $100,000,000. There can be from 40 to 100 specialty stores, two to four department stores, and, normally, parking space for 2,000 cars.

The regional shopping center is very much an integral part of retailing in the United States today and is a favorite place for national and regional chain bookstores to locate.

The Community Shopping Center

This type of shopping center is smaller than the regional shopping center, ranging in size from 100,000 to 300,000 square feet. Fifteen to 60 retail outlets typically populate the center, anchored by a suburban branch store or a junior department store. The community shopping center usually serves a market of 20,000 to 200,000 people, 90 percent of whom live within a radius of 1.25 to 1.50 miles.

The Neighborhood Shopping Center

Ranging in size from 30,000 to 80,000 square feet of selling space, neighborhood shopping centers are much more numerous than community or regional types. Five to 20 stores in the center can serve a population of 3,000 to 20,000 when the nature of the merchandise featured in the stores is virtually all convenience goods or services. Nearly always built as a strip or I design, these centers require 4 to 10 acres of land. These centers are the home of many individual, local, and national chain bookstores.

Locating in a New Building

When considering a location in a new building, it is always best to deal with a quality realtor/developer. In a commercial building you will be furnished with a lease, plan, and specifications, pinpointing the exact scope and construction descriptions of the store space. Lease specifications will stipulate the type of exterior facade, entrance, ceiling, partitions, lighting, hardware, electrical outlets, HVAC (heating, ventilating, and air conditioning), roof and insulation, plumbing, exterior walks and drives, parking, and signage rights. This outline specification will become part of the final lease. Therefore, the next step will be for the store planner to review the specifications before the bookseller "signs up."

Locating in an Older Building or What the Landlord Expects of a Bookseller

Typically, most landlords do not want details of building tenant stores to inundate them. Their standard practice is to provide a dollar contribution toward preparing the basic shell of the building to receive a new bookstore. This allowance normally applies toward architectural and engineering services, demolition, exterior facade, entrance, ceiling, partitions, lighting, hardware, electrical outlets, HVAC, plumbing, roof and insulation, exterior walks and drives, and parking. The landlord will rightfully insist on receiving and approving the plans and specifications.

Normally, landlords expect booksellers to provide the store planning services and furnish and install their own store fixtures, sales area mats, carpet and floor

Exterior, Barnes & Noble Westfarms Mall, Corbins Corner, Conn. *(Photo: Ken White)*

covering, painting, lighting, and electrical work within the store fixtures, telephones, awnings and canopies, and interior and exterior signs and graphics. Though there are exceptions to this rule, it is the normal procedure.

SITE SELECTION

With an understanding of the nature of bookstores, bookstore clusters, and locations, and with further help from the American Booksellers' Association's *A Manual on Bookselling* (3d ed., Harmony), the first step toward building a bookstore is for the bookseller to meet with a realtor and look at sites which are now on the market or will soon become available.

Here are a few tips to keep in mind when making the final choice.

- Select a site next to a highly compatible business.
- Select a site that is not vulnerable to unfriendly competition.
- Select a site with adequate parking for customers and staff, except, of course, in key city CBD locations.
- Use common sense. Ask yourself, "Is this really the best location for a bookstore in this area? Is another bookstore needed?"

Determining criteria for locating a bookstore in a new building on a college campus is a special situation and will need input from a number of administrative sources. First is the need to identify one or more (hopefully, three) available locations which for the most part:

- are readily available
- are of adequate size
- are relatively free of utilities
- are easily accessible to pedestrian and vehicular traffic, particularly delivery service vehicles
- are conveniently located in the mainstream of student traffic for both the present and future
- have access to short-term parking
- do not violate the integrity of the campus environment
- do not pose unreasonable financial burdens for construction and occupancy
- allow for the design of a modular facility to phase in with educational facility planning
- relate to long-range campus planning objectives of the university
- afford the opportunity to make a significant contribution to the total "tone and appearance" of the institution, reflecting the educational quality of the college or university
- are in a situation which will allow them to concentrate on service to students and faculty

When it has been determined that several sites meet these criteria, a site location form can then be designed by the store planner to reflect individual campus needs and to assist in determining the final recommendation. Using an instrument similar to the Summary of Site Location Factors (Exhibit 1.1), it is possible for an evaluation to be made by a number of interested students, faculty, administrative staff, and users of the bookstore and its services. This group's perception of contributing factors for each site can then be tabulated and summarized. The best site location will surface on a weighted score basis. Admittedly, not everyone will always agree, but then they never have.

EXHIBIT 1.1
UCONN CO-OP STORRS, CONNECTICUT
SUMMARY OF SITE LOCATION FACTORS
(Weighted score on basis of 100)

Location	1	2	3	4	5
1. ACCESS					
a. Pedestrian	95	95	95	80	80
b. Delivery/shipping by					
semitrailer van	95	90	70	80	80
c. Employee	90	90	70	80	80
d. Public, including vendors	95	95	85	85	85
2. SURFACE TRANSPORTATION					
a. Automobile	95	95	50	50	50
b. Bike	95	95	95	95	95
c. Bus	95	95	50	95	95
3. PARKING					
a. Present	95	95	0	0	0
b. Future	95	95	0	0	0
4. PRINCIPAL COMPETITION—DISTANCE					
a. Books	0	0	0	0	0
b. Supplies	25	25	25	20	20
c. Sundries	25	25	25	20	20
5. ENVIRONMENTAL FACTORS					
a. Impact on present physical					
plant	20	20	95	5	20
b. Influence on future planning	40	40	0	70	60
6. STUDENT CONVENIENCE FACTORS					
Relationship to:					
a. Academic Present	95	95	95	80	80
b. Academic Future	95	95	95	80	80
c. Residence halls present	80	80	80	80	80
d. Residence halls future	80	80	80	80	80
e. Athletics	70	80	80	90	90
f. Student union	70	70	70	90	90
g. Food service	70	70	70	95	95
7. SITE FACTORS					
a. Topography					
(1) Flat	80	80	20	80	80
(2) Rolling	0	0	0	0	0
8. SITE PREPARATION					
a. Sewer and water	85	80	95	95	80
b. Electric power	85	80	95	95	80
c. Telephone system	85	80	95	95	80
d. Steam	85	80	95	95	80
9. ECONOMIC FACTORS					
a. Complicity of project	90	90	50	20	80
b. Opportunity to recover					
investment	90	90	80	80	80
c. Least costly to operate	80	80	90	85	80
TOTAL	2200	2185	1850	1920	1920

SITE 1 IS RECOMMENDED

Having looked at the nature and type of bookstores, CBD, regional, community, and neighborhood shopping center locations, and referred to *A Manual on Bookselling,* you should have a good idea of where to look for, and how to select the location of, your new bookstore. Keeping in mind that the primary purpose of a bookstore is to sell books, there is still another option to consider—building your own bookstore building.

BOOKSTORE BUILDINGS

The exterior design of a new bookstore building is primarily an architectural problem. There are, however, aspects of that design problem which interface with the store planning effort. Just about everyone agrees that the characters of the interior and exterior design of a bookstore building should complement one another. The design should, at a glance, convey an image that says, "Books sold here." The focal point of the design should direct you to the main entrance of the bookstore.

Freestanding bookstore buildings assume a variety of interesting forms, shapes, and levels (see University of Minnesota and University of New Mexico plans). The creative use of shapes other than the basic box shape adds interest to selling spaces and arouses the imagination and curiosity of shoppers. Shapes can conjure up impressions of wandering through Old World stores. Many high-fashion retail shops go out of their way to create boutique forms and shapes in their stores. All this assumes that the bookstore is big enough to include the large blocks of open space needed to accommodate the bulk of the stock and which will allow for an appropriate amount of layout and merchandising flexibility.

Seattle Pacific University Bookstore Building
(Photo: Reg Hearn; architect, Henningson, Durham & Richardson, P.S.)

Except for those bookstores located in the central part of institutional buildings and shopping centers, most bookstores are neither square nor rectangular. A few minutes spent studying pages 42 through 45 will show that the shapes of stores in most situations are irregular, on biases, or shaped in the form of a T or L. Occasionally they are triangular or curved around the corner of a major street intersection.

One-Level Bookstores

A one-level bookstore has many important operational advantages, the kind you can live with day in and day out. Less staff is required, there is usually an opportunity for better customer traffic distribution, and it allows greater flexibility in planning.

Monitors and skylights, UConn Co-op *(Photo: Ken White; Architect, Galliher, Schoenhardt & Baier)*

The Medical Center Coop, Boston, Mass. *(Photo: Simeon Korisky; architect, The Architects Collaborative)*

Conveyor enclosure, The Minnesota Book Center *(Photo: Ken White; architect, Meyers & Bennett)*

Conveyor turning corner at The Minnesota Book Center *(Photo: Ken White; architect, Meyers & Bennett)*

Better visual security and merchandise control is possible, and more usable space is acquired by the elimination of stairs, conveyors, elevators, ducts, and shafts. Finally, the building will probably be less costly to construct—building codes are usually less demanding—and construction time is usually reduced for the one-level bookstore building.

In sum, new bookstore buildings should be constructed with as few levels as possible. One-level buildings do not dampen the opportunity for architectural creativity. There is great opportunity for the use of contemporary architectural design materials and monitor and skylight elements, or for the application of energy environmental systems.

Multilevel Bookstores

Multilevel bookstores arise out of the fact that either there is not enough adequate selling space available on one level to accommodate the precise need, or the building is built on a hill or rolling terrain, with entrances on two levels. Even in most one-level bookstores there may be a basement mechanical, receiving, and stockroom. Occasionally, we see the second-floor space used for offices, training, and employee lounge facilities.

Multiple levels require 8 to 12 percent more space than a single-level store to accommodate entrance ramps, special arrangements for handicapped persons, general and fire stairs, elevators, escalators, wheeler lifts, conveyors, mechanical shafts, and the additional structure required to support and enclose these conveyances and elements.

There is no functional reason why the bookseller cannot operate on more than one level. Basement, half-basement, or second-floor space is usually less expensive than ground floor space. A good bookstore planner would enjoy finding ways to make these floor spaces so enticing and interesting that people would seek them out.

Take the case of a small, three-level bookstore. One solution would be to locate the office, receiving room, employee facilities, and part of the selling area in the basement or on the second floor. The main selling area and cashiers would be situated on the ground floor. The remaining basement or second floor could be designed as a selling area with its main service desk, podiums, galleries, skylights, and other appealing devices. However, in these multilevel bookstores, a first-class conveyor or lift system is required to link the various floors together with receiving and stockroom facilities.

COLUMN SPACING AND CEILING HEIGHTS

I like to work with columns spaced 28 feet in each direction. This spacing, which results in a bay, allows for use of standard size and spacing of store selling fixtures, lighting fixtures, HVAC outlets, sprinklers, and ceiling tiles of 1-, 2-, and 4-foot modules. In most building situations, this spacing is flexible and economical.

Normal bookstore ceiling heights range from 10 feet 6 inches to 14 feet. The added inches allow space to fit and install overstock cases and larger display areas. However, ceiling heights of 7 feet 6 inches have been used on art gallery sales levels. Eight-foot ceiling heights are common in finished nonselling offices, rest rooms, and employee lounge areas. Split-level bookstores, like the Yale Co-op, or bookstores with balconies, like the Barnes & Noble Rockefeller Center Sales Annex, and Universities of New Mexico, Minnesota, and Indiana (as seen in Part Two), achieve a feeling of enormous space and acquire a special ambiance. This is achieved by partially stacking one level above the other but not fully enclosing each floor. This planning concept, however, does create multiple selling levels, which are special planning problems to deal with.

Entrance, Yale Co-op *(Photo: Freeman Payne; Architect, Eero Saarinen & Associates)*

Split-level stairs, Yale Co-op *(Photo: Freeman Payne; architect, Eero Saarinen & Associates)*

Exterior, University Bookstore, Madison, Wis. *(Photo: Wollin Studios; architect, Burroughs & Van Lanen)*

Entrance, Georgia Tech Bookstore *(Photo: Bob Geller/Visual Communications; architect, Jova, Daniels, Busby).*

Exterior, Virginia Tech Bookstore; stairs, ramps, entrance *(Architect, Carneal & Johnston and The Architects Collaborative)*

CHAPTER 2

DESIGN CONCEPTS

THE CUSTOMERS' PERCEPTIONS of the character of a bookstore are established the moment they see the store entrance and walk through the front door. Everything that surrounds the customer—the books and merchandise; the floor, walls, and ceiling; the fixtures and their arrangement—sets the stage. The colors and materials; the lighting, heating, or cooling; and the signage all combine to create the total design, atmosphere, and image of every bookstore.

This chapter will examine methods employed to create atmosphere and design themes. It discusses the use of names—local—and material to create small and large stores, and concludes with a discussion of trends in bookstore design.

CREATING A DESIGN THEME AND NAMING THE STORE

Design themes and names for bookstores are logically arrived at after a careful study of the market and location (the Asian Bookstore, the International Bookstore and Gallery, the Fisherman's Bookshop). A name or theme may be chosen that identifies a book category (the Art Bookshop; the Science and Technical Bookstore; the Museum, Judaica, or Ballet Bookshop), or the preference of the owner and a bookselling specialty may be the theme (the Chess & Bridge Bookshop, the Mystery Bookshop, the Dickens, or Literary Bookstore). All these names conjure up impressions and not only suggest a certain category of books but also an atmosphere that the bookshop will express. The most obvious, and very logical, name to give a bookstore is that of the owner or a coined name the owner has agreed to, such as B. Dalton Bookseller or Walden Bookstore.

Many bookstores dotted all over the country carry the names of their individual or institutional owner. In many cases, the name is often used as a design theme (the Gothic Bookstore), and occasionally a seal or crest of an institutional owner is made up and utilized as a trademark and becomes the basis of the interior design.

Names often used for bookstores are those of fictional or historical characters (The Oliver Twist, or Abraham Lincoln Bookshop). These shops may literally be real stage sets based on good research of the period. They will be furnished with enough period reproductions of fixtures and furnishings, as well as genuine artifacts, to carry the idea.

Occasionally a name is chosen to underscore a geographic theme (New China Books and Periodicals, the United Nations Bookshop, Europa, or the Down East Book Shop). Another class of bookstore names would be that in which the name derives from the type of merchandise itself sold or used in the store (Literary and Publishing World, the Sale Annex Bookshop, the Art and Type Bookstore, or the Paperback Bookshop). Other areas of interest can be developed into a design theme or focal point as well (the Christian Bookshop, the Design Center Bookshop, or the House of Sagittarius Book Center).

Naming a bookstore to create a design theme is like naming an infant; it is either very easy or very difficult, but the infant usually gets named whereas the bookstore

Interest in classical and Victorian styles has revived a taste for the fanciful forms and pastel color schemes of the period. These children's book department walls are framed with Victorian "portico" posts and brackets.

The University Book Store, Madison, WI
(Photo: Ken White)

Exterior, The Hammes Bookstore, University of Notre Dame *(Photo: Ken White; architect, Ellerbe Architects)*

sometimes does not. Most often this happens in airline terminals, department stores, institutions, and the like. In such cases, the bookstore is designed as a part of the building in which it is located or to which it is connected and is simply named and planned as the nonentity it is destined to become.

How does one design "atmosphere" in a bookstore? The answer is to coordinate the design of everything from the style of lettering on the facade to the style of lettering on the store bags. The general atmosphere of the bookstore must first be determined. Do you plan to attract a Beverly Hills clientele, or a Greenwich Village literary crowd? Are you going to be selling books to people keen on mysteries in a suburban town? Or will you be providing educational books and supplies for a medical school in downtown Cincinnati? Are you thinking of a brilliantly lit sale annex or a low-key book boutique? Are you planning to have Chinese cooking demonstrations in the home crafts department? And, finally, where do you plan to build this bookstore? Among semitropical Florida plantlife? On a red-brick state university campus? In the slick, sassy surroundings of Chicago's near north side? The answers to these questions will determine your proper atmosphere.

Use of Symbols and Color as a Unifying Design Theme

A symbol can be a means of establishing a trademark for a bookstore and can also provide a unifying motif throughout the design, as in some college stores. Some bookshops may use reproductions of old woodcuts and nostalgic symbols and devices as the basis of their design theme.

The use of color in some successful regional and national chain bookselling stores identifies and unifies their many shops. In fact, different areas of design, which might otherwise appear to be totally unconnected to the main design theme, can be linked to it by means of a symbol or color as the unifying motif. Such a motif can be integrated into the exterior signs, entrance, ceiling, walls, carpets, store fixtures, signage, gift wrappings, store bags, stationery, and advertising to create a unified image.

A bookstore should be thought of as a package with an interior design that visually communicates to its customers that it is a retail bookstore. The design should convey the type and quality of the bookselling establishment, because what the exterior promises, the interior must deliver.

The interior and exterior design elements and choices of materials should reflect the type and quality of books, merchandise, and services the bookstore will offer. *The character of the exterior design and building materials should be consistent with the character of books and merchandise displayed and sold.*

The image of a large, multistory general trade or university bookstore should convey to its various publics that it carries a tremendous quantity of books and merchandise, and is part of the institution. Whether it is constructed of brick, stone, concrete, or metal, its materials and design elements should reflect the character of the campus.

A small, single-story trade or college store building should meet the same criteria, though it may be rustic or contemporary, constructed of wood or a variety of exterior materials. The same criteria apply to all bookstores.

Books and Merchandise as the Theme

The high cost of rent has stimulated store planners to concentrate on maximizing the use of space in bookstores today. In Europe, because of the high cost and lack of available space, most bookstores have always stocked and displayed books and merchandise from the floor to the ceiling. Today, in many departments, merchandise has become the central theme of the decor. More and more merchandise is now brought up to or hung from the ceiling, as books, poster tracks, gifts, and soft goods' hang rods and towers are doubled and tripled in height.

The greatest number of bookstores are comprised of one selling area with a single selling environment, usually created by the merchandise itself. Indeed, the store as a whole should project one image, even though it may be a composite of the image of several floors. The range and variety of types of trade books or textbooks or mass merchandise items, such as stationery, cards, gifts, supplies, clothing, notions, and related goods, create a special ambiance all their own. Image, after all, is the result of merchandise, layout, color, lighting, graphics, and—motif.

In a large bookstore comprised of many separate areas and selling departments, each individual or major department should be designed to reflect the merchandise for that retail area. Consider, for example, how the atmosphere of a science and technology book department might compare with an electronics and calculator area. One neutral background could be used in both areas, but two distinctive environments would add up to a better image.

Science and technical books could be located in a quiet, highly visible setting with darker shades and hues reminiscent of medical, scientific, and technical library surroundings. The use of duranodic bronze, leather, wool carpets, and natural woods, with bold graphic color motifs would create a tasteful and professional environment for this department.

On the other hand, those elements might be out of place in a calculator and electronics department. A "2001" environment could be more appropriate, with a system of transparent glass cubes set on neutral-toned plastic bases and trimmed with mirror-polished stainless steel clips and locks presenting a neat solution.

TRENDS IN DESIGN

Faced with the realization that almost every bookstore has access to essentially the same titles, one comes to realize that the *difference* between one bookshop and

New York University Law Bookstore *(Photo: Ken White)*

another lies in the personality of its owner, its stock selection, the services it offers (and in fact renders), and its visual appeal. It is in this last characteristic—unique visual appeal—that independent and department store booksellers have the greatest opportunity to capture the imagination of the community they serve, and to create special bookselling places. The trend is toward more and more specialty bookshops styled with unique themes, because this approach is probably the best remaining option to use to meet conglomerate competition.

An equally strong trend has been toward a more contemporary environment in general bookstore retailing. This is because booksellers have recognized that *a more handsome contemporary atmosphere will sell more books and merchandise to today's young people*, but it does leave open a wide avenue of other design directions.

THE VALUE OF TRADITIONAL DESIGN ELEMENTS

When a bookstore opens for business, it opens its doors to people of all sorts. People tend to prefer bookstores that are warm and comfortable. Comfort arises most surely from familiarity, and the familiar to most people is traditional design. It is here that some planners take a few lessons from the traditionalists. By adapting historical and traditional concepts to the contemporary bookstore scene, it is possible to create wonderful bookstore designs with broad appeal.

It is not necessary to faithfully duplicate the architectural woodwork details of an English library, a Chinese pavilion, an art noveau Austrian shop, or a French

16 PART 1

Directoire salon (though that would be fun) to create an Old World aura. What is important is to skim off enough traditional elements to create atmosphere. Period windows, entrance doors, graphics, dark-stained or lacquered woodwork, carpeting, old-fashioned incandescent light fixtures, and a rich, authentic color scheme can be combined to create a period bookshop that is neither brittle nor delicate but, rather, relaxing and unpretentious.

CHAPTER 3

THE PLANNING PROGRAM

PREPARATION of a bookstore planning program is an organized method of directing attention to solutions that will boost merchandising and bring ambiance into new and renovated bookstores.

The planning program for a new bookstore being designed from the ground up is not very different from one being renovated in an existing building. It simply encompasses a wider range of physical factors. Since this book is intended to be useful to bookstore owners as well as to their planners, it will be helpful to explain more fully the principles of bookstore planning programs and how they come into being. They begin with the bookseller.

A bookseller should become familiar with trends, directions, and new bookselling ideas by researching trade magazines and visiting new and renovated bookstores and related businesses. He or she should talk to other successful booksellers and learn how they solved both major and minor problems. A list should be made of problems and also of the ideas, features, and expectations the bookseller holds for the new bookstore.

Another list should be compiled of all the store operating problems. Next, the *ideas, objectives, means, methods, schedule,* and *anticipated cost* foreseen for the new bookstore should be written out. The program statement need not be long and comprehensive to help clarify a bookseller's aims and to let the goal become clear. Writing out a section on each of these topics will bring into clear focus the objectives of the program. The problem and the solution are two ends of any one situation. The key question is, "What are we trying to do—what do we actually need?"

Once the bookseller has clearly outlined his or her objectives, the first step is to find someone to plan the bookstore who is in sympathy with those objectives and who has a recognizable background of retail bookstore planning. Bookstore planning differs radically from other forms of store planning and interior design. If the bookseller has not made contact with a store planner, now is the time to do so. As the client, the bookseller will now have the problem of choosing the store planner, and it *can* be a problem for someone who has never dealt with it before. One might well ask, "What is the role of the bookstore planner?"

THE ROLE OF THE PLANNER

No matter what size the project, the bookstore planner should proceed on the basis of mutual good faith to:

- properly assist the bookseller to analyze, evaluate and define his or her objectives and determine solutions in principle.

- translate the bookseller's objectives and philosophy into a planning program with attainable goals.

Good merchandising and customer service facilities that complement each other must be stated early in the planning program.

The University Book Store, Madison, WI
(Photo: Ken White)

- explore all realistic design possibilities and meet the bookseller's planning and design objectives, on time, with well-prepared, thorough bookstore construction, furnishing, and graphic plans, details, and specifications.
- aid the bookseller by attentively following the project through its construction phase to a successful grand opening.

The bookstore planner should not promise more than can be realistically accomplished or:

- attempt to exclusively conceive, plan, and design the bookstore on his or her own and attempt to force one idea or solution onto the bookseller.
- attempt to establish the bookstore's personnel, merchandising, and promotion strategies.
- set in motion the bookseller's planning requests without comment if he or she recognizes the possibility of problems unfolding.
- undertake a planning project when he or she does not have the time or professional competence to complete the assignment on schedule.

"What Kind of Planner Should I Engage?"

It often happens that a store planner has been called upon to handle the principal design of the bookstore from its inception. Occasionally the planner realizes that while the interior represents 80 percent of the project, an exterior face-lifting will require the services of a licensed architect. In this case, the planner calls in an architect who is both available and sympathetic with the design approach to handle this phase of the job. Similarly, the planner should carefully select the lighting, HVAC, and other consultants who will make up the planning team.

From the client's point of view, it is best to have any building specialists answerable to the store planner. Far more tedious, painstaking, and conscientious research, far more detailed planning, and far more field supervision are required in bookstore planning than in almost any other type of store planning and design.

Architectural and design firms are usually at a disadvantage when called upon to render professional bookstore planning and design services. Unless they are thoroughly versed in bookselling principles and considerations, their knowledge of design and construction techniques cannot be effectively applied to bookstore buildings.

When a new building or extensive remodeling of an old building is involved, an architect is needed, and in most states is a legal requirement. However, the staffs of store planning firms and increasing numbers of design firms include registered architects or professional engineers. These firms are able to handle an entire building project just as an architectural firm would.

Planning Fees   The architect is usually paid on a fee based on a percentage of the cost of the work. Store planners are more likely to work on a flat fee contract basis; architects will sometimes agree to this method of payment, too. The contract may be drawn on a lump-sum basis or may be based on a multiple of overhead and profit times the worker-hours registered on time cards and charged to the project. To this fee, normal out-of-pocket expenses are added. Either way the fees are calculated, the final cost usually ends up about the same.

One approach in deciding which way to go, then, is to look around at bookstore interiors and buildings that you feel will appeal to the type of customers you hope to attract, and ask who designed them. Then interview the firm that designed the project.

When very large projects, such as major office buildings, student union buildings, or medical centers, are involved, the bookstore will become a small tenant in a large architecturally designed complex. Store planners can do far better in this situation if they work with the architect and consultants right from the beginning. In this way, many problems can be avoided and costs often contained.

The Planning Team   Creating a planning program is more than a one-person job. The planner cannot operate in a vacuum. If the client has not already organized the planning team, now is the time to do so.

The planning team should be neither too large nor too small; while one person is not enough, 10 are too many; six is about right. Ultimately, the team for modernization or for the new bookstore building program will come from three professional areas. The first is composed of the bookseller, the bookseller's attorney, and accountant. The attorney will review leases, contracts, and legal documents before the bookseller enters into various agreements.

The bookseller should look to the accountant to help determine the general project budget, which will depend on capital available, borrowing power, and the extent of the commitment the client wishes to make. The accountant may also help the bookseller consider the types of accounting systems, cash registers, and store financial controls to be chosen. He or she may, for example, recommend that the bookstore incorporate a minicomputer. This will require space and utility connections.

From the second professional area comes the bookstore planner, the architect, and any consulting engineers whose services are required. The store planner will be about the most important person in the bookseller's professional life for some months to come. There must be as close to perfect understanding as possible between bookseller and store planner if the bookstore image, layout, and design best suited for the operation is to be achieved.

The third professional group will usually enter the project at different times. First, there will be building contractors and their suppliers. They will furnish current cost information, material samples, catalogs, and technical data. At the second stage, store fixture and graphic contractors and carpet suppliers will usually enter the picture after the store planner and architect have completed their plans for the interior and the building.

Having selected and engaged a store planner, let us move on to formalize the planning program.

THE PLANNING PROGRAM

The preparation of a planning program for a bookstore is a standard procedure. A good program can help a project run smoothly. Various store planners and their clients may use a variety of other titles (i.e., advanced planning analysis and feasibility study) to describe a particular store planning program. The size of the program document will vary with the complexity of the project. The author once made a fine program for a small bookshop that was contained on two typewritten pages; but the Advance Project Analysis Bookstore Facility for the Florida State University Bookstore emerged as a perfect bound book of some 220 pages.

In their first encounter with a store planner or architect, booksellers have a tendency to explain what they think the bookstore should look like outside and about the interior store fixtures they saw here or the cashier layout they saw there. When a store planner is engaged, the bookseller should never forget that he or she is paying the planner for a knowledge of bookstore design processes. To put this knowledge to best use, the planner, instead of being told how things should be arranged to look, should be given a detailed set of objectives, titled the program.

The bookseller should entrust the store planner with the data and statistics about the financial situation as they affect the building plans. The planner is a professional who will respect this confidence as completely as the accountant or attorney does.

Concentrating on the bookstore's merchandising plan, the store planner must become completely familiar with the bookseller's business situation. The planner must know the sales volume in every department, how this volume compares with that of the competition, and where merchandising strengths are. The planner will also need to know the kinds of customers the bookseller has and wants to have, their shopping habits, the number of customers expected to be served, and at what particular time of day. Understanding the kinds of book categories, sales merchandise, and how much stock is to be housed is also important. The strengths, weaknesses, and strategy of the competition must be studied. The client's particular display concepts, merchandise handling, service, housekeeping, and size of cashier stations, administrative offices, and employee facilities will be analyzed and tabulated, as well.

The store planner will be looking for answers to subjects like these in his or her planning conversations with the client, which is the reason why ample time should be allowed at the programming stage. Once the store planner has this information, various spaces can be planned in logical and orderly fashion.

The program should reflect intensive research on all phases of the project for large store projects. Every member of the planning team—bookseller, program committee, store planner, architect—should contribute to its form and content. Each should review and critique the work of the others. Each should be ready to carry out his or her own assignment once the program is under way. In terms of time and money, the program is vitally important. It literally becomes the bible of the project. The planning program must be sound in its original conception but flexible enough to be modified later during the preparation of the final program.

Programming the Schedule

A realistic planning and construction schedule is one of the most important elements of the planning program. Schedules may be simple (Exhibit 3.1) or detailed (Exhibit 3.2). A well-detailed schedule alerts everyone concerned to the importance

EXHIBIT 3.1
UCONN CO-OP—STORE FIXTURE SCHEDULE

	Start	Complete
Walls: Deliver	June 26	July 10
Install	June 26	July 10
Floor	July 14	July 28
Carpet	July 10	July 11
Graphics	July 28	July 29
Loose units: Deliver	July 14	July 28
Install	July 16	July 31
Refinish metal	July 7	July 19
Refinish wood	July 14	July 16
New metal fixtures: Deliver	July 14	July 18/22
Install	July 14	July 18
Complete installation	July 31	July 31

STORE FIXTURE DEPARTMENTAL DELIVERY SCHEDULE

	Wallcases	Loose Fixtures
Trade books	June 26	July 14
Checkout	June 26	July 14
Goodies	July 7	July 14
Graphic arts	July 26	July 21
Soft goods	July 26	July 21
Course books	July 9	July 21

EXHIBIT 3.2
J. NEW BOOKSELLER
OPERATION AND FACILITY PLANNING SCHEDULE

Time frame—Stated in weeks

Activity	1	2	3	4	5	6	7	8	9	10	11	12	13	14	15	JNB	KWA
1. Determine name of entity	■	■														+	+
2. Form legal entity (Corp.)	■	■														+	+
3. Select site	■	■														+	
4. Bind lease	■	■														+	+
5. Select checks—open bank account	■	■														+	
6. Reserve telephone number	■	■														+	
7. Order temporary telephone number			■													+	+
8. Request tax ID number											■					+	+
9. Retain bookkeeping service								■								+	+
10. Develop chart of accounts				■		■										+	+
11. Join ABA				■												+	+
12. Order *Books in Print*						■										+	
13. Attend ABA Booksellers School					■											+	+
14. Write and reproduce 50 copies of introductory letters to publishers and wholesalers. Mail.					■	■	■									+	
15. Contract publishers/wholesale representatives								■	■							+	
16. Open accounts with sources									■	■						+	
17. Final book list										■						+	
18. Design operating system and forms									■	■						+	+
19. Reproduce forms												■				+	
20. Design graphics and signage			■	■	■	■	■	■	■							+	+
21. Order books												■				+	
22. Prepare architectural and mechanical design documents	■	■	■	■	■											+	+
23. Bid							■									+	+
24. Award contracts																+	+
25. Prepare merchandise and store fixture plans and specifications		■	■	■	■	■											+

Responsibility

EXHIBIT 3.2 (Cont.)

Time frame—Stated in weeks

Activity	1	2	3	4	5	6	7	8	9	10	11	12	13	14	15	JNB	KWA
26. Bid						▓	▓	▓								+	+
27. Award contract									▓	▓						+	+
28. Prepare graphic statement		▓	▓	▓	▓	▓	▓	▓	▓	▓	▓	▓					+
29. Bid pylon sign						▓	▓									+	+
30. Bid and reproduce stationery, bags											▓	▓				+	+
31. Purchase interior signage										▓	▓				▓	+	+
32. Prepare systems, procedure, and policy statements									▓	▓	▓						+
33. Bid carpet and floor covering										▓							+
34. Specify equipment																	+
35. Order equipment as follows:																	
Cash registers (3)											▓					+	
Postal scale									▓							+	
Tape calculator											▓					+	
Tape shooter									▓							+	
Wrap paper and ties											▓					+	
Furniture (sales)																+	
First aid									▓							+	
Decor and graphics																+	
Book carts											▓					+	
Typewriter																+	
File cabinet—2 drawer																+	
(2) —legal																+	
Desk and chair and stools																+	
Charge plate press																+	
Charge register																+	
Display items											▓	▓	▓			+	
36. Temporary storage												▓	▓	▓	▓	+	
37. Van truck—local use														▓	▓	+	
38. Punch list																	+
39. Clean up														▓	▓	+	
40. Move in															▓	+	
41. Set up															▓	+	+
42. Preopening training															▓		+
43. Advertising				▓	▓										▓	+	+
44. Telephone hookup															▓	+	+
45. Photography				▓	▓											+	
46. Sales promotion publicity															▓	+	+
47. Grand opening (3)															▓	+	+

Responsibility

EXHIBIT 3.3
ESTIMATED START UP COST A. MODERATE BOOKSELLER

Category	Amount	
BUDGET ELEMENT A		
Professional Services		
1. Legal		
Corporate structure, lease review	$ 450	
2. Auditing		
Set up books	200	
3. Store planning		
Store plan, design, and consultation	13,279	
service including 4 trips to Fort Worth		
Subtotal		$ 13,929
BUDGET ELEMENT B		
Property		
4. Rent		
Month deposit, 1 month in advance	2,300	
5. Telephone		
Deposit	50	
6. Utilities		
Gas, electric, and water deposit @ $25	75	
each		
Subtotal		2,425
BUDGET ELEMENT C		
Construction		
7. Interior finishing		
Heating, ventilating, air conditioning,	14,000	
plumbing, lighting, painting, show		
windows, store fixture installation, carpet,		
hard surface floor, steps, podium, etc.		
8. Sales equipment and furnishings		
Store fixtures, chair lift, pass thru, book	22,190	
carts, receiving room equipment, office		
equipment, cash registers, interior signs		
decor items		
9. Signs		
Exterior pylon and building signs	8,000	
Subtotal		44,190
BUDGET ELEMENT D		
Staff and Related Cost		
10. Preopening salaries	1,250	
11. Dues and membership fees	50	
12. Subscriptions		
Reference books and professional	200	
magazines		
13. Truck and storage rental	100	
14. Telephone expense		
L. D. to follow up and coordinate	100	
project and inventory		
Subtotal		1,700

EXHIBIT 3.3 (Cont.)

BUDGET ELEMENT E			
15. Inventory		20,000	
16. Contingency		400	
	Subtotal		20,400
BUDGET ELEMENT F			
17. Advertising			
Local newspapers, direct mail, grand opening, telephone		800	
	Subtotal		800
Summary elements A, B, C, D, E, F		83,444	
Less construction allowance		10,000	
Total probable cost		73,444	

OPERATING RESERVES

BUDGET ELEMENT G		
18. Operating and fixed expense reserve		17,350
19. Sinking fund		4,575
	Total Reserves	21,925

of meeting their responsibilities—on time. Therefore, the schedule should not only define the activity that must take place but should identify the time span within which it will occur. Some schedules assign to the store planner, contractor, owner, or other person the responsibility for seeing that certain activities occur on time (see Exhibit 3.2). Further, most commercial leases include provisions requiring the store work to be completed and the store open for business on a designated date. Equally, many store leases require the landlord to meet a designated completion schedule of work. Thus, from the beginning, the bookseller and landlord commit themselves to an agreed schedule.

Holding to the schedule is extremely important for the bookseller. If store completion runs behind schedule and the opening is delayed, the bookseller can miss an entire selling season, which could knock the financial pins out from under him or her from the outset. No more devastating an event can happen to a college store. This is particularly true when the store is the sole and primary source of books and supplies as on the University of Connecticut campus.

The final planning schedule will be simple or complex depending on the size of the project. The schedule is often used as a checklist of contracts to be let and tasks to be accomplished. It is also used as a control instrument to assure that each activity is accomplished in the correct sequence.

Each schedule must be tailor-made to suit the bookstore project at hand. For example, an established bookseller will not always be faced with selecting a name for the new store, but under some circumstances, it is possible that he or she may. Exhibit 3.2 is an example of the schedule used to plan and open a 2,000-square-foot commercial bookstore in Texas.

EXHIBIT 3.4
A. MODERATE BOOKSELLER
INFLUENCE OF 800 ALTERNATE BOULEVARD SITE ON BUDGET

| Item no. | Category | Amount | | Difference |
		Old	New	
3	A. Architectural and mechanical service		$ 1,366	$ 1,366
	B. Graphic design		3,634	3,634
	C. System procedures and policy statement		2,334	2,334
4	Rent	$ 1,000	2,300	1,300
7	Interior finishing	12,000	14,000	2,000
8	Sales equipment and furnishings	21,190	22,190	1,000
9	Signs	500	8,000	7,500
17	Advertising	725	800	75
	Net increase			$19,209

Programming the Cost

The cost, obviously, will vary from project to project, and this is particularly true of a first bookstore. Therefore, the program should strive to identify *all* the cost elements involved to open the bookstore, as illustrated in Exhibit 3.3.

If alternative sites are involved in the program, the additional costs required to start up in the second location are usually identified as shown in Exhibit 3.4.

Once committed to renovating or building a new bookstore, there is a natural tendency on the part of booksellers to want to rush through the planning stage; they are anxious to see sketches and models. But time spent in clear and careful program planning will be more than made up for by the time and cost saved later. It has been proven time and again that the meticulously planned project runs smoothly.

CHAPTER 4

PRELIMINARY PLANNING

A SIMPLIFIED DIAGRAM of a bookshop would show a cube with two open ends. One would be the book and merchandise inflow; the other would attract customers. If the store is well planned, books and customers will meet in the middle. The inflow of books and their control is a complex technical process, but it holds no mysteries that can't be solved by fluent organization. The inflow of customers, on the other hand, is almost a fine art; it involves not only the best planning ability but also a smattering of showmanship and psychology. The fundamental problems are the same for the smallest bookshop and the largest store; the scale and emphasis vary. Specialized booksellers must not overlook the fact that there are basic planning principles which apply to every store.

PLANNING PRINCIPLES

The basic function of a bookstore is to sell books and related merchandise. Planning should be from the inside out. It is only after interior sales space, service areas, and equipment have been plotted and organized that a logical background exists for the design of a store's exterior facade and entrance.

The customer's attention, however, is first caught by the store front. He or she is not exposed to the attractions of the sales floor until inside. On the way in and out, customers are seldom aware of hidden service areas that are so essential from the store planner's point of view. The planner's and customer's concerns connect where the merchandise is displayed inside the bookstore.

The planner's objectives, then, are: (1) to create an efficient, attractive environment within the bookstore in order to promote maximum sales; (2) to integrate sales space with those behind-the-scenes functional service areas that supply merchandise; and (3) to attract customers into the sales space by means of an inviting store front.

Planning Problems Unique to Bookstores

Bookstores present unique planning problems because they must be designed for constantly circulating customer traffic. Customers are always browsing and on the move except at the actual point of sale and at the cash register. Store planners must give them a clear route between the store entrance and the interior sections of the sales floor. This central traffic artery should be planned so that customers can easily enter, browse, select, buy, check out, and leave. The whole pattern of sales departments should be so arranged that an attractive visual effect is obtained from any point in the interior as customer traffic moves through the store.

Bookshops may be very small or very large in size, depending on their location,

Tables, column displays and other features should be provided for in the preliminary planning stage.

B. Dalton, 666 Fifth Avenue, N.Y.C.
(Photo: Bill Mitchell)

character of merchandise, sales methods, and management. A small bookshop may be housed in a one-story space only 10 feet wide and 30 feet deep; a large store may often fill a two-story building and be 100 feet wide and 200 feet deep. The merchant in charge may be the owner of the business or a manager employed by some institution or chain store organization. In any case, and whatever its physical organization or business ownership, the bookstore limits itself pretty closely to one type of merchandise or one type of service.

Apportionment of Space

In bookstores, space is apportioned on the basis of area needed to produce a projected gross volume of sales. Data produced by the American Booksellers Association and the National Association of College Stores (Dessauer Report) are used by the astute bookseller to verify ideas and compare operating performance against national and selected averages.

For most bookshops, an annual sales goal of $100 per square foot of gross area is realistic. Comparatively, Walden Bookstores reported an average of $110 per square foot for its chain of 750 stores. In the same period, B. Dalton Bookseller sales averaged $118 per square foot of gross area. Industry rumor has it that some bookstores within these two great bookselling chains produce up to $372 per square foot, and they are probably correct.

Individual departmental sales and operational performance data, available from the National Association of College Stores to college and university bookstores for planning and comparative purposes, are the most comprehensive.

Planning the Interior Selling Space

Each category of books requires its unique place in the bookstore plan, properly related to customer traffic routes, service departments, and other functional facilities. The first step in planning is to divide and locate the merchandise to be sold into three divisions, based on the customer's point of view. These fundamental divisions are *impulse, convenience,* and *demand.*

As a rule, impulse items (including new arrivals, frontlist books, and bestsellers) should be up front and in heavy traffic spots; convenience merchandise (such as backlist books) should be centrally located; and demand merchandise (reference books) should be at the rear. Store layout should require customers to walk through as much of the store as possible to reach items they plan to purchase. This will give customers the opportunity to see other books and merchandise. Similarly, each category should have within its display area convenience, demand, and impulse locations.

Size and Location of Departments   The following factors are used to determine the size and location of selling departments within diversified trade bookstores:

1. The departmental sales forecast (goal)

2. An estimate of how many units of merchandise each department must have on the floor to reach the volume goal

3. The type of selling to be used: personal selling (pens, expensive books), selling from sample (engraved stationery, imprinted Christmas cards), self-service (general books, supplies, art materials, novelties, gifts, etc.). These variations affect choice of fixtures, provision of space for customer movement within the department, amount of space to be allocated to feature displays, etc.

When the selling space has been allocated, the store planner calculates the space needed for nonselling activities with equal care.

Location of Merchandise   To make it easy for the customer to find a book or to shop for related merchandise, book categories and nonbook departments should be placed in logical relation to each other, in a shopping pattern that does its own suggestion selling: Art near Photography, History near Sociology, Cooking near Hobbies and Home Repair. However, it is not always possible to do a complete job of lining up related categories or departments, partly because of differences in sales productivity per square foot, and partly because of sheer physical limitations.

The planner can increase sales by cross-merchandising departments also: for example, athletic equipment in the sports book department, and live plants or packaged seeds in the gardening book department. There is an interesting and effective trend evident in the direction of "minishop" or "boutique" locations—a particular group of books or style of merchandise is collected from several departments and presented in a visual merchandising display to appeal to a particular kind of customer. Even the smallest shop can be planned with this visual merchandising principle in mind. In larger stores, it is one of the cornerstones of successful retailing.

Controlling Traffic

Many psychological factors can be used to control customer in-store traffic patterns, and the professional store planner always strives to incorporate them. For example, it is a fact that as many as 90 percent of the people entering a bookstore tend to move to the right. And they naturally gravitate toward a brilliantly illuminated, brightly colored area. These known factors should be used to encourage an easy flow of customer traffic into and throughout the store, exposing people to the maximum amount of merchandise. Placing a continuous row of tiny decorative light bulbs on a wallcase cornice or painting a rear wall with a strong color, for example, will help pull customers from the entrance door to the back of the shop, creating opportunities along the way for impulse purchases.

The Entrance   Whether or not to provide an entrance area is largely a matter of choice although, in cold regions, it does become almost a necessity. The entrance area may be a simple opening from a covered mall, or it may consist of a vestibule. An entrance area has several functions: It can give a sense of spaciousness to a bookstore (even to one which is rather small) and can provide a meeting place for customers. It can also be the first inside statement of a theme suggested by the exterior and can act as the introduction to a bookstore's amenities. A small bookshop may only have room for a vestibule, but even this small space can provide opportunities for a designer to create a good first impression of the bookstore. It is

Entrance, Contract Design Center Bookshop, Chicago, Ill. *(Photo: Hedrich Blessing)*

desirable that the customer receive a general impression of the entire interior while still in the vestibule or as he or she steps off the stair, elevator, or escalator on an upper floor. The design of an entrance should reassure a customer. A well-planned entrance ensures easy exit and entry.

Entrances must be located so that delivery truck traffic will not interfere with the flow of customer traffic. Once customers are inside the bookshop, it is the function of the indoor sales area to expose them to as much impulse merchandise as possible.

Aisles and Circulation   The amount of aisle and circulation space planned for customers and staff depends on the type of bookstore. The size of the sales floor will determine whether there will be a single aisle or several aisles. In a small bookstore, a straight, dead-end aisle may be all that is possible. In bookstores with larger floor areas and more complex merchandising programs, a centralized main aisle will have branch aisles to disperse shoppers through the sales area. If the store is very large, the main aisle should be paralleled on one or both sides by other aisles. These aisles should be connected by a pattern of cross aisles and by one or more main cross aisles.

Main aisles 5 to 7 feet wide allow some degree of aisle merchandising. When this space exists, it is good to place a sale table or tables in the middle of the aisle. The space between the aisle selling fixtures and wall units should be 3 to 5 feet. Cross aisles 4 to 5 feet wide are desirable. In many situations, aisles are frequently narrower by about 10 to 15 percent.

Customer comfort must be carefully considered when determining aisle widths. It is good for a bookstore to sometimes be crowded, but a customer who is jostled and feels closed in or lost will usually want to get out of the bookstore as quickly as possible, and more important—not come back!

Delivery entrance, Minnesota Book Center, Minneapolis, Minn. *(Photo: Ken White; architect, Meyers & Bennett)*

University of Connecticut Coop, Storrs, Conn. *(Photo: Ken White; architect, Galliher, Schoenhardt & Baier)*

Entrance, Anderson College Bookstore, Anderson, Ind. *(Photo: Ken White)*

Brigham Young University Bookstore.

Entrance, Loyola University Bookstore, New Orleans, La. *(Photo: Ken White)*

Main stairs, B. Dalton, 666 Fifth Ave., New York City *(Photo: Bill Mitchell; architect, Alfred Nelson)*

Escalators in show window, B. Dalton, 666 Fifth Ave., New York City *(Photo: Bill Mitchell; architect, Alfred Nelson)*

Vertical Movement The problem of circulation is of utmost importance for stores having sales areas on several levels. Well-designed and inviting stairs can overcome the customer's objections to walking up or down. Customer stairs that lead to other selling levels require special design attention. One device is to mirror them in such a way that the sales displays on the other floors are visible all the way up or down.

When locating vertical transportation for customers, it is preferable that stairways and escalators be placed about two-thirds of the way back in the selling area, thus exposing the customer to most of the main floor before leaving it for another level. In addition to customer stairways, enclosed fire stairs and exits are usually required. Local building codes and ordinances must be checked on this point. Fire exits must be planned so they lead directly to the exterior.

Impulse Buying Although more and more attention in general retailing is being given to capturing impulse sales, the average bookstore—planned on hit-or-miss lines—has barely scratched the surface of this opportunity to increase volume. Scientific store planning and merchandising help take full advantage of every square foot of sales space to capitalize on impulse buying. The economic success of a store can depend on how well it stimulates these impulse sales. If a store sold only demand or convenience merchandise that its customers had planned to buy before they entered the store, it could soon be in bankruptcy. Buying surveys by one major bookselling chain have shown that over 50 percent of all book sales it rang up were impulse sales. This means that their customers made more than half their purchases without having planned to do so before entering the store. Every store's newspaper advertising of staple merchandise and bargain sales promotion is calculated to bring in customers seeking demand or convenience merchandise.

Sales floors organized to take advantage of impulse buying can provide comfortable, convenient shopping conditions for their customers. Easy traffic routes and attractive sales departments help to make shopping fun. When customers find that it is easy, convenient, and fun to shop in a bookstore, they will come back again and again.

Cashier Stations and Service Desks Finding the best location for a cashier's station is always a problem. If at all possible, cashiers should be placed on the left side of the entrance for small bookstores. Why? Remember that traffic flows to the right on the way in and does the same on the way out.

Cashier stations and service desks can create a lot of traffic disturbance during rush hours, if they aren't carefully planned. The policy of the bookstore will decide the functions and services of the cashiers. When the basic function is to ring up transactions and make charges, small L-shaped checkout units or straight counters are usually satisfactory. Bookmarks and impulse sales can be conveniently conducted from the cashier station if the bookstore retails any of these specialties and they are displayed at this point.

Other service functions, such as receiving payment on charge accounts, making charges, special ordering, accepting telephone orders, layaway, and gift wrapping require larger cashier stations. Very large stores may relegate these activities to service desks located elsewhere in the bookstore.

Some nonselling functions, such as special order and information desks, can act as a magnet and draw customer traffic to interior locations in the bookstore. Knowledgeable store planners purposely locate these customer services in the rear or even on upper or lower floors. Provisions must be made at service desks for microfiche readers, reference books, storage space for books and merchandise awaiting customer pickup, store telephone and paging instruments, and an appropriate quantity of reserve bookshelves and files.

B. Dalton, 666 Fifth Ave., New York City.

Receiving Rooms and Stockrooms

The relationship of the receiving and marking room to the sales area is of utmost importance. It may be contiguous to the sales area in a small bookshop or located three selling levels away in a very large store. In some unusual arrangements, merchandise is received in a central receiving facility and then delivered to the bookstore. When this happens, the receiving process consumes more time and is more expensive than in the standard, adjacent flow-through arrangement.

Wherever possible, stockrooms, like receiving rooms, should be located immediately adjacent to the selling area. There are several methods open to the store planner for determining stockroom locations. The perimeter plan is most widely used in college bookstores. The central service core plan is most often found in general bookshops. The imaginative planner can usually design a combination of these plans to effectively handle movement of merchandise.

It is fairly obvious that the number of customers to whom the sales area caters should not be greater than the receiving room can comfortably handle at the most rushed period. If the receiving room is larger than necessary, space and equipment is wasted; if it is smaller, then errors, short tempers, and any number of other crises are inevitable. How much receiving room space to allow will vary with the amount of inventory to be processed, the size of the bookstore, variety of the merchandise, and frequency of deliveries.

Since receiving room space is nonincome-producing, it is essential to keep it to a minimum. But at the same time adequate space must be provided to open, unpack, count, check, and verify the price of incoming books and other merchandise. Provisions must be made to file shipping documents and process return shipments. A "hold" area for books and merchandise awaiting pricing or other processing information is essential, as is storage space for a reasonable quantity of store bags, supplies, and used shipping cartons kept on hand to facilitate returns.

Receiving room, Bucknell University Bookstore.

The Staff Lounge and Rest Rooms

Small bookshops generally have one rest room, a drinking fountain, and a coat rack or bank of employee lockers. Larger stores require greater amenities. A properly

Perimeter stockroom, Minnesota Book Center
(Photo: Ken White; architect, Meyers & Bennett)

sized employee lunchroom, often with a kitchenette, drinking fountain, pay telephone, and coat lockers, is routine. Separate men's and women's toilet rooms with an employee "nap" or rest room is required by many local health and building codes. Few bookshops build special public rest rooms.

BASIC BOOKSTORE PLANS

The concept for formulating the overall interior layout of the bookstore selling areas is based on statistical data, merchandise requirements, intuition, and professional experience. The most popular types of bookstore plans are the *open grid plan*, and the *angular plan*, or *zone and cluster plan*.

The Open Grid Plan

The open grid plan consists of a completely open sales space surrounded by perimeter wall fixtures with center floor sales fixtures laid out in parallel and repetitive

Staff lounge, Minnesota Book Center *(Photo: Ken White; architect, Meyers & Bennett)*

Raised gallery, Barnes & Noble, Westfarms Mall, Corbins Corner, Conn. *(Photo: Ken White)*

Books Underground, consecutive galleries, Coffey Hall Bookstore, University of Minnesota *(Photo: Ken White)*

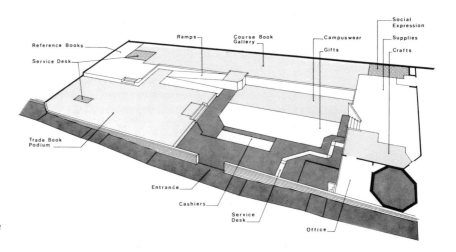

arrangements. Department divisions and selling fixtures are usually kept at or below eye level. If any of the sales equipment is high, it should be of a see-through type to permit visibility throughout the bookstore. The open grid plan is most commonly used by mall, chain, and general bookstores.

The main advantage of this concept is that it provides flexibility, lower building cost, good visibility, an opportunity for merchandise exposure, cross merchandising, and security for the entire selling floor. The main disadvantage of the open grid plan is that it restricts the opportunity to create a sense of place and atmosphere for book departments. As a result, we see disconnected merchandise relationships.

Raised Galleries and Podiums   The visual problem of the open grid plan, however, can be reduced by raising selected departments and merchandise classifications to an appropriate height and onto a raised gallery with levels varying from 8 inches to 4 feet. Consecutive galleries, raised one level above the store, can also be used for greater efficiency in use of space and to create more interesting plan arrangements. Merchandise capacity is increased and security is improved when a raised department is clearly separated from its neighbors. In larger stores, galleries at the far ends of the space let you know where shoppers are. Customers on the gallery also see the store and its merchandise from a different perspective, and the potential for visual selling is upgraded.

Access for the Handicapped   Federal and many state laws require that access be provided to all selling and service levels of college bookstores. It is also a matter of consideration for our fellow humans. Inclined ramps with a ratio of a 1-inch rise to 12-inch lengths and steps with safety handrails meet federal guidelines. They are used for customer and functional access to the galleries.

The Angular or Zone and Cluster Plan

The need in larger stores to provide some definition between major book categories and nonbook merchandise departments has led to the popularity of the angular or zone and cluster plan, in which secondary and side aisles are not perpendicular to the main aisle. The concept is to cluster each major category of merchandise in zones and thread them together with a main aisle to move traffic in a counterclockwise direction. Within each zone, loose floor fixtures and displays are angled to facilitate the traffic flow and related product categories are clustered to create special visual merchandising situations. This concept permits greater flexibility and latitude of design treatments in the individual zones. This concept works well with either perimeter or centralized service core stockroom plans.

Access for the handicapped, Books Underground, St Paul, Minn. *(Photo: Ken White; architect, Meyers & Bennett)*

Locating Categories and Departments within Angular or Zone and Cluster Plans   Locating merchandise in the front, center, rear, or sides of the store in the angular or zone and cluster plans should be based on the need for an item to be exposed in a primary location for customer convenience and for stock and capacity requirements, and on an item's impulse sale value. High-impulse merchandise is best located around entrances, service desks, and cashiers, which are the most heavily trafficked areas and where customers congregate.

The ability of various departments to produce a target dollar sales volume differs dramatically. Some compact departments, such as film and processing or calculator sales, deliver above-store averages for the square footage space occupied.

Departments with greater area demand and support requirements are usually placed further from the entrance and on either lower or higher levels. The location of large departments, or of convenience, would fall into this consideration.

Nonselling facilities, such as administrative offices, service desks, employee facilities, and related areas, are always placed in secondary locations. The receiving department and stockrooms should relate to the sales area and also to the account-

Record gondola, Brigham Young University
Bookstore.

Anderson College Bookstore *(Photo: Ken White)*

ing office to facilitate the flow of paperwork. Placement of nonselling areas will have a considerable effect on the shape and use of the selling departments that surround them.

The B. Dalton Bookseller store described in Part 2 of this book is an example of angular planning and the U Conn Coop is an example of a zone and cluster planning concept applied to a full-service bookstore.

MODERNIZATION PLANNING

The initial step in preparing a floor plan for existing space is to measure the exterior shell of the space, and the location of the entrance, stairs, and utility rooms. These measurements are then reduced to an "existing condition plan," drawn to scale. Where existing fixtures are to be reused, they must be measured, surveyed, and plotted in on the plan drawing. Thus, the plan prepared will provide a clear view of the layout. The conceptual planning process is virtually the same as it is for a new bookstore. The detailed planning work involved in bookstore modernization, however, is tedious, time-consuming, and often complex.

Techniques of Gaining Space

With careful, imaginative planning, extra stock capacity can usually be found for books and merchandise. Several techniques employed are to extend wallcases to the ceiling, thus increasing shelf capacity. Book and merchandise gondolas may be double-decked and glass cubes can be built around columns. The use of book beams, the technique of extending stock shelving down from the ceiling to a height of 7 or 8 feet above the floor, not only adds increased capacity but contributes to the character and image of the bookstore interior.

Occasionally, wallcases are placed against the face of wall projections, such as

HVAC ducts, building pilasters, and pipes, and considerable space can be gained by moving them flush against the building wall between the projections. Spaces between fixtures can be equipped with appropriately selected slotwall or slatwall merchandise displays, which add to the selling power of the area. In other situations, these spaces can be covered with mirrors to visually stretch the size of the space.

Converting to Self-Selection

For college stores, a major space-gainer can be the change from clerk selling to self-selection. With this popular concept, the floor area, which was formerly occupied by sales clerk aisles, counters, and showcases, is released for customer browsing and selling. Increases of 20 to 30 percent in individual stores sales volume have been attributed to this type of conversion.

The Sizes of Things

Poorly sized equipment may be consuming from 25 to 30 percent too much floor space—for example, the use of 30-inch-wide trade book or record gondolas where the job can be done in 24 inches; or 24-inch-deep window etageres and wall apparel fixtures that really only need 16 inches of depth.

The size and location of offices should be carefully reviewed, and the cost of relocating return air ducts, controls, and other devices which are taking up valuable wall space should be looked into.

It is feasible to occasionally develop additional storage space in a bookstore with a high ceiling by building a mezzanine stockroom directly above areas occupied by existing stockrooms. Constructing a balcony space over part of the selling area is another option.

Trade book gondolas, Princeton University Bookstore *(Photo: Freeman Payne)*

Planning for Security

Theft of books is a serious problem. It has been believed for some time that the best form of theft protection is an alert staff, attentive to all potential customers entering the bookstore. This continues to be true for most small stores. But as the size of bookstores has expanded into large and multifloor configurations, the cost of staffing large and often remote areas has soared. At the same time, shoplifting has increased over 50 percent during a recent 5-year period, according to the FBI's Uniform Crime Report, with one person in 15 entering a retail store to steal.

The store planner's role is to arrange a comfortable traffic flow and spatial environment which does not impede store security. For small stores, the planner has the option to use raised checkout, office, and sales areas,[1] or controlled fixture layouts and galleries.[2] The same principles apply to the planning of large stores such as B. Dalton, 666 Fifth Avenue,[3] and Books Underground.[4]

Visual surveillance of the sales floor by the staff logically calls for low center floor fixtures, approximately 4 feet 6 inches high. But as stores generate more sales volume there is a constant need to stock more titles. The result is that selling fixtures become taller, which in effect creates a series of cul-de-sacs, often with high esthetic appeal but poor security.

Where a control or security problem is anticipated, mirrors, closed-circuit cameras,[5] uniformed guards, and electronic surveillance systems can be employed. With these devices, shelf heights can be increased and additional merchandise displayed

Window trade book etagere, University of Chicago Bookstore *(Photo: Freeman Payne)*

[1]See Barnes & Noble.

[2]See Contract Design Center, Store 9, Part Two.

[3]See B. Dalton, Store 1, Part Two.

[4]See Books Underground, Store 14.

[5]UConn Co-op, Part One.

for additional sales volume. Electronic surveillance systems are popular with libraries and an increasing number of independent, chain, and college bookstores. They are reported to reduce shoplifting by as much as 80 percent. In operation, customers simply walk through a gateway in the proximity of the store's exit. If books, and indeed other merchandise, have been rung up properly, the customer exits smoothly from the sales area. But if the books or merchandise have not yet been paid for, a sensing unit is activated, sounding an audible alarm alerting store personnel. The system is activated by a strip of magnetic tape inserted in the spine of books, or by magnetized tags applied to general merchandise. This system is also used for screening personnel entering and leaving the store.

More freedom in the arrangement of aisles to lead customers past impulse items into shop arrangements, and higher stack areas are possible with electronic surveillance systems.

HOW I PLAN A BOOKSTORE

I have given you a picture of how space is apportioned, and discussed methods for locating categories and departments within the store, and types of bookstore plans. The most practical way to help the reader understand the principles of the store planning process is to tell how I personally set about the job of planning a bookstore and, in passing, to say if my methods differ greatly from others that I know.

Block Merchandise Planning

Using the program as the script, or the scenario, I begin by making a "breakdown" of the space. This involves deciding how much area will be assigned to each selling and functional space within the area available. This important step in the planning process involves determining the amount of wall shelving or hanging capacity that the blocked-out area will accept. The remaining space in the department is then calculated mathematically to determine the number of appropriate store fixtures the remaining area will contain, after provisions are made for customer and service aisles. This is where properly sized modular building column bays become so important. There is a school of planning thought that skips over this step and goes directly to the layout and arrangement of the store fixtures and service facilities from the block plan. The weakness of that approach, however, is that the planner might find himself or herself without adequate capacity at the end of the plan and have to start over again.

Final sizes of departmental areas are then sketched and blocked out onto several building plans drawn to ⅟₁₆-inch, ⅛-inch, or ¼-inch scale. These plans relate the adjacency of one merchandise department to the other, in several combinations, to determine the best visual and operational flow. They naturally relate the nonselling and service areas with the sales area.

An efficient overall design is based on a smooth, workable traffic layout. A floor plan that is forced in order to develop a particular motif can turn into an operational nightmare. Unfortunately, there are many examples of poor bookstore planning where the novelty of an idea seen elsewhere was adopted, resulting in wasted space and unnecessary footsteps.

Several block plan layouts are always prepared, all drawn to scale. It is then possible to review and discuss several possible planning solutions. When the block plan has been established in the horizontal plane of the store, I study the possibility of dramatizing the selling area by raising or lowering one or more departments. Changes in level will finally be accomplished by building raised galleries or sinking plaza areas using normal construction methods in specially selected departments.

Although the element of cost is most important, before moving on to the preliminary store fixture planning, it is advisable first to seek the ideal solution, almost

Electronic surveillance system (*Photo: Courtesy of 3M Company Security Systems*)

without regard to eventual costs. Adjustments can always be made to keep within the limits of a reasonable cost budget.

The Preliminary Store Fixture Plan

With the departmental adjacencies established on the block plan and the ideas reviewed with our client, the next step in the planning process is to lay out and arrange the preliminary store fixture plan. This is the plan where store selling fixtures, equipment, and service requirements are drawn in merchandising arrangements within the shapes and boundaries of the selling departments determined by the block plan. It is, of course, necessary to take care to order, arrange, and draw the preliminary store fixture plan so the distances are correct to accommodate the customer aisles, the required number of appropriate sales fixtures, and the quantity of shelving required to house the amount of stock planned.

Overlays   In thinking out a plan for a bookstore, I try to imagine the people that will be using the store, and I ask myself, "How will they perceive it?" I begin sketching the preliminary store fixture layout by working out the main areas—first with rough plans ⅟₁₆ inch to the foot in scale on buff-colored sketching tissue, and then at ⅛-inch or ¼-inch scale. These sketches are known as *overlays*.

As the preliminary overlays are worked out, we must determine the height of any selling area to be raised up onto galleries and any changes in the height of ceilings. As one cannot always visualize measurements exactly, I have a 2-inch-wide surveyor's rod (rule) running up the wall beside the door of my drafting room. This is divided into 1-foot sections in alternating colors with the footage nicely numbered. It is tremendously helpful in deciding such things as whether a cornice or an overstock fixture should be 7 feet high or 10 feet high. The rod helps us visualize the comparative height of the store fixtures which will border the raised galleries. Because more merchandise is visible and accessible, main merchandising action usually takes place deep in the store at the point where major customer aisles intersect. These points become the locations for employing imaginative visual merchandising concepts such as endcaps, steps, slotwall, or similar features. All the best ideas on the overlays are collected, neatly sketched, and lettered onto a single finished plan drawing.

The Preliminary Plan Drawing

With the basic merchandising plan concept set and the sales and service areas established, thought and effort turns to coordination of the plan with the ceiling arrangement, changes in ceiling height, beams, valances, curtain walls, lighting, HVAC outlets, sprinklers, and the store fixture equipment plan. The final preliminary plan will order and merge ramps, galleries, store fixture arrangement, and major traffic arteries into a single statement. This is illustrated in the plans of the Hickory Stick Bookstore, Washington Depot, Conn.; Barnes & Noble Bookstore, the Centereach Mall at Long Island, New York; Seattle Pacific University Bookstore, Seattle, Wash.; Mt. Sinai Medical Bookstore, New York City; the main floor of Valdosta State University Bookstore, Valdosta, Georgia; Barnes & Noble Sale Bookstore, Boston, Mass.; Jigger Shop Branch of the Princeton University Bookstore, N.J.; Trinity Beacon Bookstore, a Christian bookshop in Deerfield, Ill.; and the Bucknell University Bookstore, Lewisburg, Penn., the most financially successful small college store in the country. These plans are seen on the pages that follow.

Models   As the preliminary plan is developed and drawn, I find it useful to make a study model of the bookstore interior and occasionally the exterior. These study models are often very rough, made of cardboard with departmental spaces and aisles colored in, but they are useful in many ways. They help to verify the ideas we have

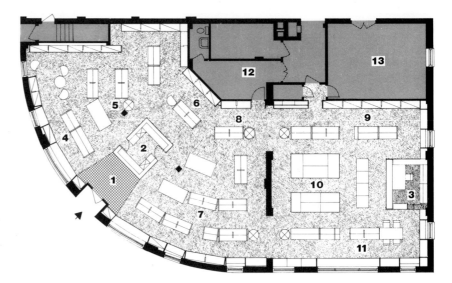

The Hickory Stick Bookstore, Washington Depot, Conn. (1) Entrance; (2) service cashier desk; (3) raised office; (4) nonfiction; (5) fiction; (6) art; (7) paper bound editions; (8) games and puzzles; (9) children's books; (10) cards; (11) stationery.

Barnes & Noble, Centereach Mall, Long Island, N.Y. (1) Front entrance; (2) rear entrance; (3) service desk; (4) manager; (5) children's gallery; (6) main gallery; (7) bestsellers; (8) cooking; (9) general fiction—nonfiction and sale books.

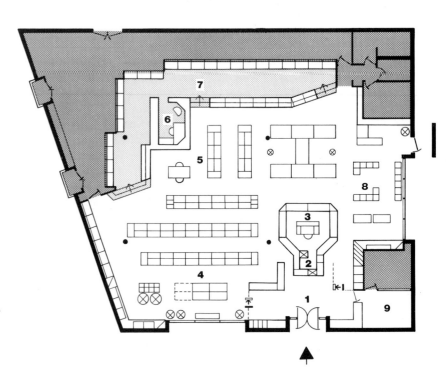

Seattle Pacific University Bookstore, Seattle, Wash. (1) Entrance; (2) cashiers; (3) controlled sales; (4) supplies (5) trade books; (6) raised book department and manager's office; (7) course book gallery (8) gifts and novelties; (9) manager.

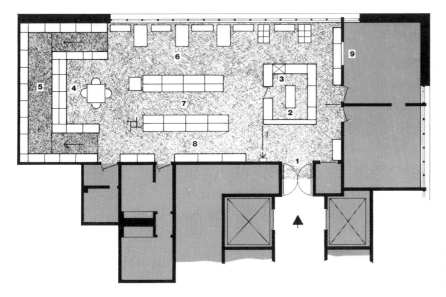

Mt. Sinai Medical Bookstore, New York, N.Y. (1) Entrance; (2) controlled sales; (3) cashier; (4) medical reference books; (5) medical course book gallery; (6) trade books; (7) supplies; (8) soft goods; (9) manager.

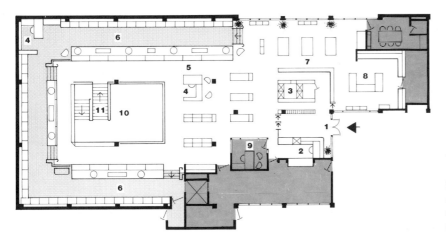

Valdosta State University Bookstore, Valdosta, Ga. (1) Entrance; (2) service desk; (3) cashiers; (4) book service desks; (5) reference books; (6) course book gallery; (7) trade books; (8) stationery; (9) open well; (10) stairs to lower selling levels.

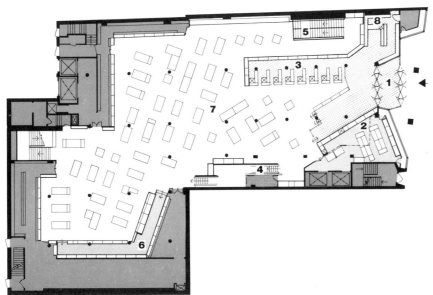

Barnes & Noble Sale Bookstore, Boston, Mass. (1) Entrance; (2) book and parcel check; (3) cashiers; (4) escalator to 2d floor; (5) stairs to lower level; (6) children's gallery; (7) general sales area; (8) buy back and service desk.

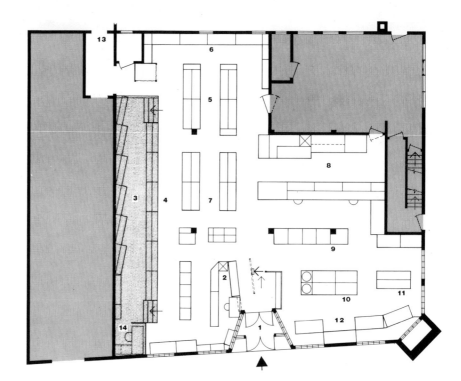

Jigger Shop Branch, Princeton University Bookstore, Princeton, N.J. (1) Entrance; (2) cashiers; (3) general book gallery; (4) course books; (5) athletic goods; (6) soft goods; (7) school supplies; (8) sweet shop (fountain); (9) room furnishings; (10) cards; (11) art supplies; (12) records; (13) rear entrance; (14) manager.

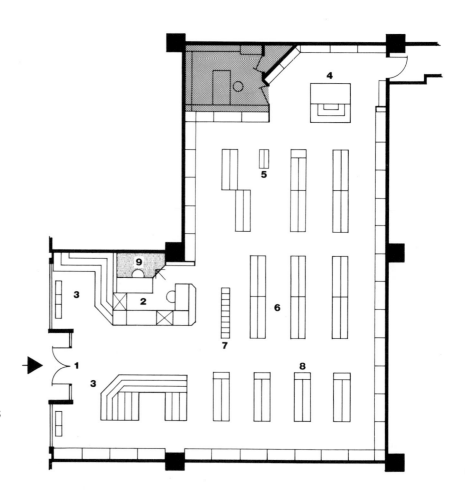

GPO Bookstore, Los Angeles, Calif. (1) Entrance; (2) cashiers and service; (3) new arrivals; (4) browsing table; (5) art prints; (6) general books; (7) cube quantities; (8) endcap feature sales; (9) manager.

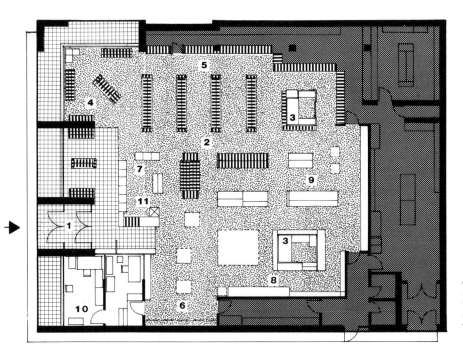

Trinity Beacon Bookstore, Deerfield, Ill. (1) Entrance; (2) trade books; (3) service desk; (4) reference books; (5) course books; (6) campus wear; (7) gifts; (8) social expression; (9) supplies; (10) office; (11) cashiers.

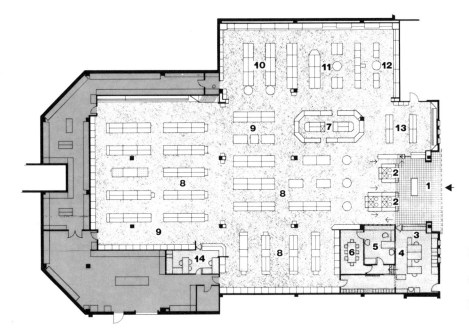

Bucknell University Bookstore, Lewisburg, Pa. (1) Entrance; (2) cashiers; (3) service desk; (4) office; (5) general manager; (6) conference room; (7) controlled sales; (8) trade books; (9) text books; (10) sportswear; (11) cards; (12) gifts; (13) sundries.

and give a bird's-eye view of what the store will look like. These models are particularly handy for studying traffic flow and the relationship of sales equipment to the structure of the building, especially if the space is populated with a forest of columns.

Because models bring the plan into three-dimensional form, they help achieve good planning balance and are an aid in studying the visual design composition. Later in the planning process, as the design development proceeds, I like to have the study models brought up to date and will incorporate into them finalized motifs and graphic design elements. The number of models required is a matter of scale. Three were required for the Contract Design Center Bookshop, but 15 models were needed for the B. Dalton New York City store.

Occasionally, larger scale models are made to study special types of store fixtures, graphics, and complex and sensitive design problems.

Rendering Perspective Sketches   Design perspective sketches are a part of the process and a means to an end. Store planners and designers constantly collect and sketch out informal ideas as they travel—at meetings, lunches, or, in my case, on trains or airplanes going from one project to the next. These little "noodle" sketches are drawn on whatever is at hand—napkins, business cards, flight coupon jackets, or in notebooks or diaries, for the next step and later reference.

As the plan is developed, I find it helpful to sketch out a number of bird's-eye views and normal perspective sketches of the principal aspects of the bookstore. These sketches are made to visualize the way the elements of the plan and the design will relate to the program and to one another. Many design sketches are simple line drawings, but others are a combination of ideas and portray the contrasting qualities of each of the bookstore design elements. They preview the development of the character and ambiance of a section of the bookstore.

Many of the perspective design drawings made by our staff of designers are very beautiful. The designers work with a number of design and drawing styles. Their presentations range from a casual collection of delineated plans, line sketches, and color boards to finely detailed, richly colored, shaded rendered elevations and perspective sketches.

Some bookstore projects require detailed perspective sketches with every shelf drawn in place in order to convey to the client the scope of activity which will occur in the scene illustrated. These sketches are often reproduced and used by booksellers to assign bays and shelves to plan the location for basic book categories.

Perspective sketches are drawn in a variety of art mediums. Black line shadow and tone sketches are most commonly made because they are easily reproduced and are used for advertisements, publicity, and a host of other purposes once the final design is established. Some designers prefer to draw with colored ink, pens, markers, and washes. Still others work with Conte crayons on colored paper or make full-color illustrations with pastels, water colors, or tempera colors. Illustrations are intended to capture the spirit of design, are often imaginative, and always impressive. Some design drawings are true works of art.

Updating the Preliminary Plan Estimates

With the preliminary store fixture plan, the model, and sketches made, the next important step is to review and update the estimate of costs and the time schedule to complete the planning, building, and opening of the new bookstore. This is serious work and often requires securing preliminary estimates of both cost and time from reliable fixture and specialty contractors. This procedure is a safeguard both to control cost and keep the project "on target." If cost is excessive, this is the time to adjust the preliminary plans and scope of the work to bring the whole thing back onto budget.

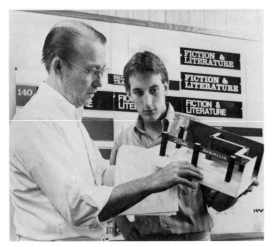

Author and designer Jeff Tyler studying model.

Selmer Drolsum, B. Dalton construction coordinator; author; and Frank Browne, NICO construction superintendent, using model to visualize project.

Duke University Medical Bookstore.

Entrance study, Seattle Pacific University Bookstore.

Proposed bookstore, University of Notre Dame.

Trade books, Anderson College Bookstore.

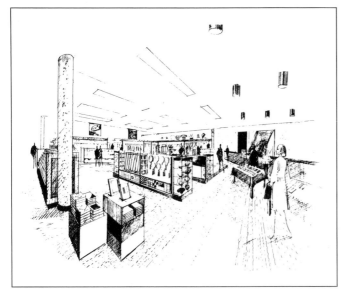

Sporting goods department, Duke University Bookstore.

Sale book department, Your Bookstore.

Entrance, Musty Ole Book Dept., Varsity
Bookstore, Lubbock, Texas.

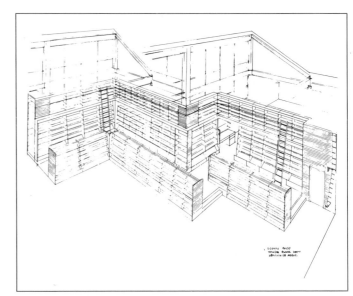

Trade book wall study, University of Connecticut
Coop.

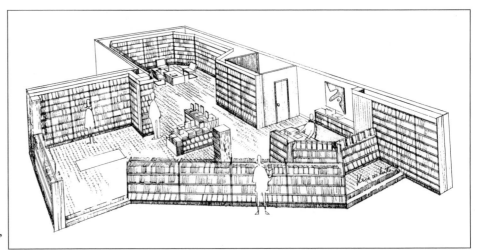

Science and technology department, B. Dalton,
666 Fifth Ave., New York.

Presenting the Plan

When the preliminary plan has been thought through to a conclusion and agrees with the planning program, it is presented to the client along with the model or sketches, the finish schedule describing the materials contemplated, the updated budget, time schedule, and status reports.

The presentation sometimes requires the presence of the project architect, and always the bookseller's planning team. This meeting is important. Here, the first decisions are made which will affect the client's well-being for a very long time. At the conclusion of the meeting, the bookseller should be able to advise the store planner, architect, and others to proceed with the design of both the exterior and interior of the new bookstore. This is also the time and place to make any suggestions or changes which will affect the plan. In this way, everyone will be certain of what the budget includes and of the proposed construction schedule of the project.

Final definite plans, specifications, and details may be simple or complex. They are necessary in order to obtain competitive estimates and to start actual construction. Each bookstore planning project is a unique undertaking. The final plans and specifications will incorporate and specifically detail all the elements of the bookstore design—the subject we examine next.

CHAPTER 5

DESIGN ELEMENTS: WALLS, FLOORS, AND CEILINGS

WALL AND COLUMN TREATMENTS, flooring ceiling, lighting, color, graphics, and store fixtures constitute the elements of bookstore design.

There are countless combinations of bookstore design elements which give the store planner the opportunity to establish an overall sense of visual unity within the bookstore. With such a variety of elements, the store planner can literally create a bookstore of any image, quality, character, level of drama, and excitement.

This chapter should make the bookseller aware of the principles which govern that part of the planning process where the determination is made to use a particular material, finish, or texture for the largest and most visible surfaces in the sales area. It sets forth the idea that materials and textures selected should not only be in harmony but should be chosen to reflect visually those traits that best portray the bookstore image.

The chapter begins with information on two of the most important surfaces in a retail bookstore—the walls and columns. It then describes the most popular flooring materials for bookstores, and discusses types and features of the materials of the largest surface area exposed to customers—the ceiling.

WALL AND COLUMN DESIGN ELEMENTS

The character and image of each individual bookstore determines the amount and location of free wall space in the entrance and in the selling area. Bookstores committed to a strong book image will probably cover building walls from floor to ceiling with bookcases right up to the entrance. Wall spaces behind cashiers, on exposed end panels, and around columns will usually be covered with wood paneling or treated with slotwall. Slotwall is a flexible system of narrow, thin, Plexiglass shelves fitted into snug grooves cut into plywood panels. At other times, columns may be mirrored, plastered with a smooth or rough texture, or enclosed with drywall board and painted. Occasionally, columns are covered with a textured vinyl fabric, felt, or wallpaper in a color and design appropriate to the theme.

The same principles apply to other nonbook sales merchandise departments. The character of the retail enterprise will determine whether the back wall of the stationery and gift department, or the wall space above greeting card fixtures, will be mirrored, paneled with wood, upholstered in felt or fabric, or lined with perforated hardboard and painted a harmonizing color.

The quality and merchandise strategy of the bookstore will determine if, for example, posters and banners are to be displayed in rolls, opened out, or hung from the ceiling; or if soft goods and clothing are to remain folded flat, or displayed and sold on hangers. To a large degree, these merchandise considerations will control

Quarry tile, parquet floors, carpet borders, wall graphics, and ceiling and lighting should be in harmony to best portray the bookstore's image.

Barnes & Noble, 18th Street & Fifth Avenue, N.Y.C. (Photo: Ken White)

Textbook wall treatment, Indiana State University Bookstore, Terre Haute, Ind. *(Photo: Ken White; architect, Archonics Corporation)*

Trompe l'oeil end panel, Loyola University Bookstore, New Orleans, La. *(Photo: Ken White)*

Changing theme at a breaking point, Loyola University Bookstore, New Orleans, La. *(Photo: Ken White)*

Creating natural barriers with frames and baffles, Brigham Young University Bookstore.

the design decision to paint, panel, or otherwise treat the wall spaces in the selling area from the floor to the ceiling, or the narrow band between the top of the selling fixture and the ceiling.

In long, narrow stores, the strip wall space above the selling fixtures can be made both interesting and practical by relating the color, material, texture, design motifs, and graphics to the merchandise displayed below.

It is a good idea to hold to the minimum the number of different textures and design ideas used on these strip wall surfaces. Too many different design elements can be distracting and will overwhelm books and merchandise on display.

Changing Themes

It is a good idea to separate each change of theme at a natural breaking point: a column, corner, or cornice. When no natural divider exists, the planner can create one with a frame, baffle, or trim member. The important thing is to be sure that each individual element contributes to the total image of the sales area and builds and reinforces the character of the bookstore.

For the walls of the book departments, the best idea is to let the books themselves be the texture and theme of the design.

Popular Textures for Bookstore Interiors

The illusions which can be created with standard building textures are boundless. Following is a helpful checklist of textures.

CHECKLIST OF BOOKSTORE INTERIOR FINISH TEXTURES

- STONE—SLATE—QUARRY TILE—TERRAZZO

- MARBLE—CERAMIC TILE: matte, glazed, handmade.

- BRICKS and PAVERS: common, old, face, new, patterned, glazed, painted.

- WOOD and WOOD PANELING: (beams, moldings, lattice strips), rough, smooth, polished.

- CARPET: rolls, tiles, tufted, woven, cut pile.

- PLASTIC LAMINATE: matte, shiny, metallic, splattered, textured.

- METAL: (hardware, trim, graphics), dull, brushed, reflective.

- CORK: (floors, ceilings, walls), roll, sheet, tiles, smooth, cut, bark.

- FABRIC: (walls, flags, draperies, tents).

- WALL COVERINGS: cotton, linen, grass and silk cloths, flocked, printed, vinyl coated, wallpaper.

- LEATHER: (flooring, upholstery, wall covering), suede, rough, smooth, tooled, tufted, glazed.

- VINYL FABRIC: (walls, columns, ceilings), rough, smooth, metallic, dull, shiny.

- PAINT: smooth, rough, sand finish, matte, semigloss, gloss, rolled, brushed, sprayed.

- PLASTICS: (graphics, screens, light diffusers), clear, transparent, tinted, colorless, opaque, smooth, textured, dull, glossy.

FLOOR DESIGN ELEMENTS

It is a fact that in all bookstores a great deal of the floor surface is covered by displays and selling fixtures, but a certain percentage of open areas and aisles remains to be seen by customers. Therefore, extreme care must be exercised to see that the floor material, texture, and color does indeed contribute to the overall image and character of even the smallest bookstore.

The prime considerations for choosing floor covering materials are the contribution to the unity of the total image; the order of the space; and the decorative quality, initial expense, and maintenance requirements.

Characteristics of Some Flooring Materials:

Quarry and Vitreous Tile Composition: Hard-burned, impervious, solid clay floor block. Thickness: various—⅜ inch to ½ inch. Color: various. Qualities: smooth and textured, hard surface, resistant to staining by impurities, chemical acid. Cove and bullnose shapes available; attractive and sanitary. May be thinset in latex.

Magnesite Composition: oxychloride inorganic cement; one brand includes copper. Thickness: ½ inch. Color: various. Qualities: smooth, monolithic. Same hardness as hardwood. Good resilient working surface. Highly water-resistant, nondenting, wear-resistant, nondusting, vermin-proof with copper.

Vinyl Asbestos Tile Composition: vinyl resins, asbestos, and pigments. Thickness: ⅛ inch. Color: multicolored or monochromatic. Qualities: unaffected by alkaline moisture, mild acid solutions. Resistant to cigarette burns; resilient. May be used above, on, or below grade.

Brick Pavers Composition: solid clay and pigments. Thickness: ⅝ and ¾ inch. Color: multicolored or monochromatic. Qualities: long-wearing, extremely resilient. High resistance to indentation. Brick pavers are laid in epoxy or cement grout. May be used on concrete floors above and below grade.

Cork Tile Composition: pure cork compressed to provide good wearing qualities. Thickness: 3/16, 5/16, and ½ inch. Color: light to dark tans. Qualities: extremely quiet

EXHIBIT 5.1
POPULAR FLOORING MATERIALS FOR BOOKSTORES

Materials	Appropriate Areas of Use							
	Lobby	Steps	Rest Rooms	Sales Area	Office	Receiving Room	Employees' Lounge	General Storage
Concrete	Yes	Yes	No	No	No	Yes	No	Yes
Quarry and vitreous tile	Yes	Yes	Yes	Yes	No	Yes	Yes	No
Magnesite	Yes	Yes	Yes	Yes	Yes	Yes	Yes	Yes
Marble/slate	Yes	Yes	No	Yes	No	No	No	No
Vinyl asbestos tile	Yes	Yes	Yes	Yes	Yes	Yes	Yes	Yes
Sheet vinyl	Yes	Yes	Yes	Yes	Yes	Yes	Yes	Yes
Brick	Yes	Yes	Yes	Yes	Yes	No	Yes	No
Cork tile	No	No	No	Yes	Yes	No	Yes	No
Wood	Yes	Yes	No	Yes	Yes	No	No	No
Carpet	Yes*	Yes*	No	Yes	Yes	No	Yes	No

*Do not use if there is exceptionally heavy traffic in the area.

and very resilient. May be used on any smooth concrete or wood surface above grade.

Wood   Composition: strips, squares, or plank. Thickness: various. Colors: wide range. Qualities: handsome, good resilience, but high maintenance. Appropriate in areas of hard wear. High resistance to indentation. May be used on a concrete floor above grade; with a good vapor barrier, it may be used on or below grade but only if manufacturer approves installation.

Carpet   Carpet for bookstore sales area use should be of a contract quality, popularly priced, and guaranteed. There are a number of reliable carpet mills which manufacture carpet to meet this need; most are centered in the South.

The quality of contract carpet used in most bookstores must pass a Class B flame spread rating of 75 or less. Usually, three plies of yarn are constructed into tufted level loop carpet, through a polypropylene primary backing, and to this, a second jute back is adhered. Carpet is normally made in 12-foot widths and the largest rolls average about 100 linear feet in length. Seaming and joining the carpet presents no problem to skilled carpet installers. They lay it flat on floors and bend it up on walls, over steps, and across platforms and galleries. Ceilings are also known to be carpeted.

Wide ranges of surface appearance and textures, plain or striped, are available. Most large mills make carpet styled in the currently popular heather colorations, including the most demanded earthtones, as well as those dramatic colors that will enhance any bookstore. These carpets have a naturally low static propensity.

Many commercial carpets are performance certified by the makers of the yarn used in the making of the carpet. The Badische Corporation guarantee is simple, specific, and reads in part, " ... if the surface of the carpet wears more than 10 percent within five years from date of initial installation, the fiber maker will replace the affected area with equivalent carpeting at absolutely no cost to you. Note that the guarantee is nontransferable and applies only to carpeting for which wear, if any, is not attributable to negligence or burns, casualties, cuts, pulls, and the use of improper cleaning methods or other causes beyond the control of the fiber maker. The guarantee does not apply to carpeting placed on stairs or to carpeting under desk chairs, where chair pads have not been used. This guarantee applies only to commercial grade carpet as defined." (Stratton Carpet Company.)

Specialized Floor Covering   Each type and color of floor conveys a certain image which should be in keeping with the overall atmosphere of the bookstore. The suitability and proportions of each floor covering material in any bookstore interior will be determined by the type of building, its location, and the use, intent, and character of each area in the particular bookstore. Each material, properly selected, will contribute its part to the total image and success of your bookstore.

CEILING DESIGN ELEMENTS

A properly designed and coordinated ceiling can add significantly to the bookstore interior atmosphere. More ceiling area is exposed to customers than any other surface in a bookselling area. Though people generally do not walk around most bookstores looking at the ceiling, the customer sees literally thousands of square feet of ceiling area in a large bookstore.

In many bookstore building projects, the largest amount of construction work is within the ceiling. Before the ceiling can be installed, the HVAC (heating, ventilating, and air conditioning), electrical, sprinkler, telephone, sound system, and other utility lines must be properly located, installed, and tested. Only then can the finished ceiling surface be installed.

The magnitude of the ceiling in most bookstores requires that the surface material chosen be appropriate to the design theme of the interior. If ceiling beams or graphic elements, store fixtures, valances, or design motifs are to be secured to the ceiling, structural supports must be provided.

Space permitting, the ceiling may be raised or lowered over selling or service areas, departments, or shops to emphasize selected spaces.

The ceiling conceals the HVAC, electrical sprinkler, and sound systems at B. Dalton, 666 Fifth Ave., New York City *(Photo: Bill Mitchell)*

Wood slat ceiling, Books Underground, St. Paul, Minn. *(Photo: Ken White; architect, Meyers & Bennett)*

Exposed concrete ceiling, Minnesota Book Center *(Architect: Meyers & Bennett)*

Modular metal and concealed spline ceiling, Contract Design Center Bookshop, Chicago, Ill. *(Photo: Ken White)*

Materials

There is a wide range of materials available for construction of finished ceilings. Each conveys a different image and adds a special contribution to the interior environment. Just as wood slat ceilings convey one image, high gloss and reflective mirror ceilings create another. Back-lighted stained glass ceilings add to the mood of a nostalgic setting, and a skylight effect over a customer stairwell or escalator adds sparkle to a contemporary store image.

Square edge, lay-in acoustical tile is the most common ceiling used in commercial store buildings today. The store planner and bookseller also have available concealed spline textured acoustical tile; wood slats; modular metal, plastic, or glass mirror squares; cork, plaster, drywall, and plain and vinyl-covered modular ceiling tile to create the proper bookselling atmosphere.

Acoustical materials are conditioned by legal restrictions in certain metropolitan areas; for example, in Class I buildings, fire-resistant materials must be used throughout; in Class II, 50 percent of materials may be combustible, but not to exceed 3,000 square feet.

Acoustical mineral tile comes in both plain and fissured surfaces. Paint (other than waterbase) causes appreciable loss in sound-absorbing efficiency.

Perforated acoustical tile comes in both fire-resistant and combustible forms, in several thicknesses for varying conditions, and it can be painted repeatedly.

Meanwhile, bookstore planners, architects, and designers are beginning to combine ceiling materials in new ways with other functional elements so that all may contribute to this important design surface.

Exposing the Ceiling

There is, of course, the design option to omit a finished ceiling and expose the structure and utility lines. Exposing wood rafters in a barn, attic, or loft conveys one image. Planning for an exposed steel or concrete structure is another. Leaving the ceiling and a cobweb of pipes exposed in a basement, painting the pipes an eerie lunar green, and extending it over a children's department is still another. It's not what you do that counts—it's when and how you do it that is important.

Ceiling color is as important as surface texture and design treatment in the design of a large store and department store shops, because it unifies selling spaces. However, the vastness of the typical off-white ceiling can act as a foil for areas painted in colors which contribute to each decorative departmental theme.

Lay-in modular ceiling tile, Barnes & Noble, Westfarms Mall, Corbins Corner, Conn. *(Photo: Ken White)*

CHAPTER 6

BOOKSTORE FIXTURES

THE BOOKSTORE FIXTURE PLAN determines whether or not a given amount of store fixtures will fit into a department and a complete bookstore. The plan will indicate where wallcases, gondolas, towers, and sale tables are located. It will indicate how many clothing racks, spinners, endcaps, step displays, and stacker boxes will comfortably fit into a space and where they will be placed. The fixture plan also dictates sales fixture size. If, for instance, the distance between a column and a wallcase measures 11 feet, then the fixture selected for that spot, whether it be a sale table, four-way rack, or wirebound book pallet, cannot be wider than 3 feet after allowing 4 feet for two aisles. The same reasoning holds true for every store fixture chosen for that particular location.

FIXTURE DESIGN

It is important that bookstore sales floor equipment be carefully designed or thoughtfully selected for the part it has to play and for its contribution to the overall image of the bookstore. Otherwise, both bookseller and customer will find it difficult to recognize either a clear-cut logical plan or well-organized merchandising presentation. The end purpose of planning for bookstore fixtures is to provide the best possible equipment for stocking and displaying merchandise, transacting sales, and providing customer service—all at minimum cost and maximum sales results.

Featured decorative pieces have a right to be elaborate or fussy, but basic bookstore fixtures are a means to an end. The moment the basic fixtures become overly elaborate, they dominate their merchandise and detract from its sales appeal.

Proportion, line, form, finish, and function are all important in selecting store fixtures—and the toughest to describe in words. What we are after are well-constructed and well-designed fixtures. That is why the bookseller should rely on the planner for recommendations. Only a trained eye, experience, and repeated exposure can teach that lesson.

The best way for a bookseller to acquire an instant lesson in good equipment design is to make several trips to bookstores of varying quality. This will demonstrate more about fixture construction and the difference between quality and shoddiness than can an entire book. Visit a good quality bookstore and browse through the various sections and departments. Examine the store fixtures. Notice the type of shelves and shelf suspension systems, the case materials, and the luster of the wood grain finish. Study the design and appearance of the fixtures. Spend at least an hour absorbing the atmosphere of the bookstore.

The next stop should be a visit to the most expensive retail bookstore in your area for the purpose of observing the store fixtures and the manner of their installation. Try to decide what makes them so appealing. Is it the way in which they display the merchandise? Is it the beautiful combination of carefully selected colors,

Store fixtures should be selected to suit the need, purpose, style, proportion, character, and type of bookstore in which they are used.

*The University Book Store, Madison, WI
(Photo: Ken White)*

finishes of the fine wood grain, or the hardware? Is it the quality of the store fixture installation? Or is it all these qualities?

Next, take a trip to the bookstore selling the lowest quality of books and sidelines. Go through the same motions of shopping and observing. Notice the quality of the materials used. Look at the fixture frames, backs, bases, shelves, lighting, and end panels. Study the periodical racks, hang rods, and checkout counter. The difference between good and bad proportion, between quality and shoddy construction and installation, and good versus inferior workmanship should become glaringly apparent.

The purpose of these expeditions is twofold. First, the bookseller will become aware of some of the differences between types of bookstore fixtures and the manner in which they are installed. Second, he or she will come to discern good proportions, balance, and symmetry; the materials and finishes—in short, the overall appearance of bookselling equipment. Once quality and design have been recognized, good judgment concerning store fixture value follows naturally.

Modular Fixture Systems

A module is a unit of architectural measurement. Thus, wallcases, gondolas, and theme tables which are 5 feet long are referred to as "built to a 5-foot module." If the store fixture happens to be made with two bays, or sections, the phrase "bays on a 30-inch module" is used.

Four feet is the most common building module today. Floor, wall, ceiling, and lighting fixtures are standardized in multiples of 1 foot. Except in very special situations, such as sale annex bookstores, 4-foot-wide store fixture modules and bays should be avoided. For one thing, the shelves will sag under the weight of book and supply stock. For another, the module is too wide to accommodate the sectional division of book classifications in most bookstores.

Five-foot-module bookstore fixtures are compatible with the building module. They too are based on increments of 1 foot and neatly tie in with standard building finish materials.

The point of all this is that for economy and practical purposes, as many as possible of the fixture bodies, or shells, should be the same module (size). This will permit interchangeable interior merchandising equipment—shelving; inserts for children's and art books and pamphlets; hand rods; crossbars, faceout displays, and drawer cabinets—to be moved from one store fixture to the next. The use of standard module dimensions reduces the number of spare shelves and other parts, and simplifies their storage. This flexibility allows store staff to easily move entire sections and departments either from one wall to another, or else out onto the center floor.

In summary, modular fixtures require less initial investment, are adaptable to a greater variety of merchandising shifts, and will contribute to the order and atmosphere of your bookstore.

SELECTING THE PROPER MATERIALS

Practically speaking, it is nearly impossible to proceed with the selection of fixtures without evaluating the advantages and disadvantages of the various materials and finishes available. The store fixture manufacturing industry today utilizes a wide variety of the four primary materials—wood, metal, glass, and plastic—to fabricate and assemble an enormous number of different kinds of store fixtures. Indeed, some store fixtures are made entirely of any one of the four primary materials.

The number of techniques employed in the assembly and construction of store fixtures varies from plant to plant. Not every plant is equipped with electronic glue edgers, for instance, and most depend upon slower, more costly methods of bonding and finishing plywood and particle board edges. So the use of a particular kind

Modular wall fixtures, Rizzoli, Georgetown *(Photo: Ken White)*

of material in the construction of store fixtures can be almost as important as the material itself in judging the potential life span, upkeep, and appearance of the unit.

Certain needs are nearly universal regardless of the use of the store fixture—shelf adjustment, drawers, and locks, for example—and the construction of the store fixtures will determine *if* and *how* those needs are met.

Wood

Solid Wood   Wood and wood products are one of the most important building products used in fabricating fixtures. There are numerous species of softwood and hardwood available, though oak, walnut, and mahogany are more traditionally related to and popular with booksellers when natural wood fixture finishes are required. Poplar (white wood), sugar pine, and birch, finished with lacquer, enamel, or paint, are the woods best used for long spans.

Plywood   Plywood is a versatile material—it is available in flat sheets, curved shapes, and can be bonded to metal and other wood surface materials. It is strong, durable, can come with fireproofed qualities, and is a stable material. With tight grain face veneers such as birch, plywood may be readily painted or laminated with plastic veneers. Plywood is most frequently used for shelves, case ends, drawer fronts, and occasionally entire bookstore fixtures.

Synthetic Wood Panels   Particle flake or chipboard has gained universal acceptance and came into use as a substitute for plywood panels. High-density particle board is reasonable in cost, easy to work with, and readily accepts paint, lacquer, or laminate finishes. Synthetic wood panels with plastic laminate facings are used in bookstore fixture work for fixture backs, step units, end panels, sliding doors, and other applications. This material should not be used when material strength is critical, as with bookshelves—which will sag and remain that way. Properly used, however, this material can cut fixture costs and be of service for years.

Wood and plywood floor fixtures, Rizzoli, Georgetown *(Photo: Ken White)*

Metal

Think of all the places metal is used in constructing bookstore fixtures and you will conclude that no bookshop or college store could be built today without using metal in some form. In fact, some attractive bookstores are fully equipped with metal store fixtures—not necessarily book fixtures, but fixtures just the same.

There are a number of metal fixture systems on the market today. I have not been able to find one that completely fills the bill, though I have found, and use, one wonderful metal component—bookshelves. These are thin, strong, and durable. When painted in an appropriate color, the shelves blend into the book jackets and are not perceived as metal. They are inexpensive and a good buy.

One of the major national bookselling chains is currently experimenting with and has gained a high degree of success with a nearly complete steel bookcase system, a combination of metal and simulated wood trim members. Hopefully, the system will be available to all booksellers in a few years.

Slotted chrome-plated metal tubing is a versatile metal suitable for many bookstore applications. The tubing, assembled with snap-together fastenings, lends itself to use in show window etageres, gift and stationery towers, book build-ups, and soft goods and supply item displays. Virtually all clothing displays are made of metal with plated finishes.

Large, thin sheets of metal can be laminated to plywood, and are useful for fabricating overhead and show window treatments. In fact, stainless steel, aluminum, brass, and bronze sheets, with polished or brushed finishes, are available in laminate form. Properly used, they can enhance the esthetic qualities of fixtures and the total atmosphere.

Glassware towers, University of Connecticut Co-op *(Photo: Ken White)*

Metal course book fixtures, University of Connecticut Co-op *(Photo: Ken White)*

Metal wall supply cases, University of Connecticut Co-op *(Photo: Ken White)*

Tote and handbag merchandisers, University of Connecticut Co-op *(Photo: Ken White)*

These same metals are found in store directories, handrails, hardware, displays, and a host of other places. Steel, the most workable of all the metals, can be plated or finished with baked or air-dried lacquer and epoxy coatings.

Glass

Illustrating the rule that "form follows function," glass cube fixtures have emerged on the bookstore scene. Held together with a system of metal or plastic clips, squares or rectangles of glass are arranged, complete with hinges, hasps, and locks, to form open or closed glass boxes in a variety of intriguing functional forms and arrangements.

Glass cubes are used to solve a variety of merchandise problems. Small cubes are perfect for displaying gifts and glassware. Cotton goods can be organized and displayed in medium-sized cubes. Longer 20-inch-square glass cubes, mounted on base storage cabinets, are replacing glass showcases in hundreds of retail stores. The application and arrangement of glass cubes is limited only by the imagination. I have stacked 20-inch-square cubes four high on a wood base around the four sides of a column with great success. Glass cubes appear to have earned a place of their own in the bookstore.

Metal soft goods merchandisers, Books Underground *(Photo: Ken White)*

Metal-framed camera self-selection cases, Brigham Young University Bookstore.

Glass soft goods cubes, University of Connecticut Co-op *(Photo: Ken White)*

Mirror and glass cubes, University of Connecticut Co-op *(Photo: Ken White)*

Adjustable shelves in endcap, B. Dalton, 666 Fifth Avenue, New York City *(Photo: Ken White)*

Shelf inserts, children's bookshelf, University of Connecticut Co-op *(Photo: Ken White)*

A glass security door and lock added to individual cubes adds a new merchandise dimension. Glass cubes can be used to display fine, expensive bindings and art books; typewriters and dictation machines; calculators and cameras; and are an excellent value for the money.

Cubes are best made of tempered glass, which provides a modicum of personal protection if it should be broken. When tempered glass breaks, it shatters into relatively harmless fragments.

There is a pronounced increase in the use of plate glass mirrors in bookstore design and fixture work. Glass mirror is used to reduce column size, to expand the size of small spaces, and for security. Float glass is used for glass shelves, showcases, and sliding doors in gift, stationery, supply, notions, and clothing departments. Plate glass is the quality glass which continues to have many uses in bookstore fixture work, including show windows and glazed doors; as well as for skylights, partition walls, and fixture work.

Plastics

Where are we today with the use of plastics in bookstore fixture work? Plastics have gained a reputation as a viable fixture material in several categories.

Tough, hard, transparent Plexiglas and Lucite come in a wide variety of sizes and thicknesses and are relatively easily worked. They lend themselves to cutting, drilling, and heat form bending. Plexiglas is frequently specified by bookstore planners for category sign holders and book easels; display cube steps and risers; large, transparent clothing racks; and counter bases. Plexiglas would be a wonderful material to use for a science fiction bookshop, utilizing its range of interesting, transparent colors. In their many forms, these and other plastics are translucent or opaque, as well as transparent, and, last but not least, the majority are reasonable in cost.

The second class of plastics which I use in fixture work is of the molded variety. Colorful plastic tables and stackable bookshelves; storage bins and cubes; door pulls, hinges, and other hardware are tough, durable, and good buys.

Plastic upholstery and wall covering—waterproofed and flameproofed—are successful indoors and out.

The third category, high-pressure laminates, have been with us for years. They were originally made in a $\frac{1}{16}$-inch thickness for countertop use. Today, we have both that and $\frac{1}{32}$-inch vertical grade laminates, which may be bonded by plastics manufacturers to a high-quality particle board, core, or panel. These factory-laminated panels are available in a variety of thicknesses and range from up to 5 feet wide to 10 feet long. Neither plastics nor high-density particle board are dirty words in the bookstore fixture world. They are common quality materials, perfectly satisfactory when used in the proper manner. A wide range of colors and nearly perfect wood grain imitations, photographically reproduced, are available in this durable, long-wearing surface material.

FIXTURE FLEXIBILITY AND ADAPTABILITY

In the long run, it is important to be able to adjust to changing times and keep up with merchandising trends and directions. The ability to do this influences the design and selection of fixtures and their flexibility and adaptability. The most basic element of flexibility is the adjustment of shelves.

Adjustable Shelves

Bookshelves are best suspended from their ends. This eliminates the possibility of damage to book jackets caused by shelf supports located midway along the shelf. Two rows of support brackets are normally used for trade and reference books, but three rows are a must for deep textbook shelves. In some instances, the weight may be so great that it will cause the support to fail.

Adjustable angled and flat supply department shelves are supported from the back at each end.

Individual wood and glass adjustable shelves are usually supported from the back on adjustable "knife" brackets supported by a metal standard, fixed to the fixture back or finished wall.

Shelf Inserts

With the addition of a wide variety of display inserts for children's and art books, periodicals, outlines, memo books, graph paper, and monograms, the bookstore can have nearly total flexibility and be as simple, economical, and attractive as you choose it to be.

Hangware

Hang rods and crossbars, adaptable for waterfall faceout bracket highlighting, mount on the same type of wall standard as do glass shelves. Metal standards are occasionally used to support cornice light brackets which contain the lighting elements to illuminate wallcases.

Refinishing, Remodeling, and Reusing Fixtures

It would be ideal for everyone if we could begin planning every bookstore from scratch. For most bookstores, that will not be the case. We will have to incorporate existing wallcases, gondolas, theme tables, checkouts, service desks, and accessories into the new scheme. This complicates the planning and the project, but most existing fixtures can be blended into a new plan with success.

If the fixtures are made of metal, they can be painted with an electrostatic finish. If there is an eclectic collection of wood fixtures, they can be painted or one of the many kits on the market can be used to give them an antique finish. Counters can be cut down and a new high-pressure laminate applied to worn and scratched tops. Chipped and scratched glass showcase tops and shelves are easy to replace. However, the cost of labor is so high that the cost of a renovated store fixture beyond refinishing can cost nearly as much as replacing it with a new one. But by refinishing old fixtures and rearranging them in a new plan, it is possible to obtain a fresh, new image.

On the other hand, if some of the older fixtures are fine pieces, thoroughly functional, and worth retaining, there is another option. If they were expensive to begin with and could not be replaced today at the same price—and are too valuable to be painted—I would simply incorporate them into a new scheme.

My approach here would be to develop a plan of some ingenuity incorporating those fixtures in an imaginative layout. I would surround the fixtures with a bold color scheme, which would cause them to become secondary in importance. I would adjust the lighting scheme to shift visual emphasis away from the fixtures to the background. This technique can transform a dowdy sales area into one that is warm and friendly.

The Life Expectancy of Fixtures

The life of quality bookstore fixtures during their use is surprisingly long. In a recent analysis of 120 bookstores which I planned between 1955 and 1970, I found that the majority of the basic equipment was still in place and in use. Virtually every bookstore had been remodeled to some extent and a small percentage of the equipment had been lost in the process. But the good news was that the main inventory

Art periodical shelf inserts, Contract Design Center, Bookshop, Chicago *(Photo: Ken White)*

Hang rods and crossbars, University of Connecticut Co-op *(Photo: Ken White)*

of the equipment was intact. By this time, the equipment in these bookstores has more than paid for itself, regardless of how much was originally paid for it.

Fixtures, regardless of their price, should be practical, easy to maintain, and able to stand up under constant use. If a fixture looks poorly made or feels rickety to begin with, 6 months of use will probably finish it off. Such a piece of equipment has no place in a quality bookstore.

TIPS ON SELECTING FIXTURES

Here are some tips to bear in mind when selecting fixtures:

- Consider the function or purpose of the fixture. Will it be moved? Must it be adjustable? Is it adaptable to more than one category of merchandise? What finishes are available?
- Consider the problem from a merchandising angle. Will the fixture expand your creative options? Should it be lighted? Does it require special signage? What is its size?
- Keep an open mind. Chrome and glass etageres make wonderful window and tower merchandisers but so do colorful plastic and natural wood units. Don't restrict your thinking.
- When selecting mass-produced fixtures, verify sizes, materials, and construction methods used. Turn the fixture over. One look at the bottom and back will tell a lot.
- Think about maintenance. These fixtures will be with you for years.
- Don't limit your merchandising plan to one style of fixture. Good design cuts across style boundaries. A mixture of styles gives the bookstore scheme variety and a unique touch. An unusual breakfront, or exceptional chairs at a browsing table, can become a decorative tour de force.
- Don't overspend and overequip. Follow your planner's advice.

BUDGETING

Bookshop and college store fixtures and selling equipment represent a considerable investment. It takes the largest bite out of most bookstore interior building budgets and, therefore, merits careful thought and selection. The four primary questions to ask when buying fixtures are:

1. For what merchandise will it be used?
2. How will it be used?
3. Is it a good value?
4. Is it needed—will it increase capacity and sell merchandise?

Budgetary considerations will determine whether a given fixture represents the best value for the price. Clearly, fixtures selected and recommended for one bookstore will vary with the next, based on a store's character and budget. Today, every bookstore is planned and (hopefully) built "within budgeted cost." Easy to say but sometimes difficult to achieve. Value is the key word. Are the fixtures selected the best value for the amount paid?

Looking for Value

Value cuts across all styles and types of bookstore equipment. Whether a piece is made of wood or metal or plastic, it has a value depending upon your budget. Moderately priced stock equipment lines generally include a host of mediocre, badly designed fixtures that are overpriced for what they offer in the way of construction and materials. The pitfalls of low-priced fixtures are their claims to be something which they are not. The danger in buying a cheap fixture lies in its poor construction and shoddy use of materials.

The fixture plan tells us what types of fixtures we need, the quantity required, and the correct size. The store planner's experience and the bookseller's personal preference tell us what kind of fixture to look for. Well-designed and constructed fixtures and sales equipment represent a good value with the price commensurably higher.

There are several approaches for determining how much you should spend for fixtures, and what kind you should buy. Each has merit. The first approach stresses the importance of purchasing only high-quality fixtures that will render lasting service through the term of a 10-, 15-, or 20-year lease. These fixtures represent an investment.

The second approach calls for the purchase of basic quality stock store fixtures, supplementing them with a number of "trendy" display and sales devices considered expendable. This approach is successful in bookstores requiring seasonal store fixtures which complement an overall atmosphere and relate to other merchandise lines.

A third approach is to design, build, and install low-cost equipment that suits the merchandising purpose at hand and disregards the idea of fixtures as an investment. This type of design and construction has its place in bookstores where the aim is to create a no-nonsense atmosphere. These interiors can be as successful as any other because they do not pretend to be anything but what they are. This type of fixture is acceptable provided booksellers know just what they are getting for their money.

SOURCES FOR EQUIPMENT

Quality bookstores and their planners are notoriously secretive about revealing the names of the manufacturers of their store fixtures. This explains why so few of the manufacturers' names are known to booksellers at large. Your planning consultant can furnish you with the names of firms with which he or she has had good experience in all parts of the country. The planner will also be able to provide you with reliable sources for the standard specialty items you will need from time to time.

Industry publications list advertisers who make several grades of bookstore fixtures. From these firms, you can obtain catalogs and order one fixture or an entire store. If you have not actually seen the equipment which you ordered, be prepared for disappointments. Quality and production control are two of the store fixture industry's major headaches. Few moments are more frustrating than when you receive a long-awaited store fixture—only to find it does not come up to expectation. Dealing through the planner with a manufacturer you trust can reduce this possibility and make the acquisition of fixtures less of an ordeal.

It is a good idea to order fixtures as far in advance as possible. Long delivery time is another fact of life. Bookstore fixtures have a delivery period that varies from 3 to 6 weeks after the order is placed; during the late summer when all related stores are pressing for installation materials, the delivery period can extend as long as 10 to 12 weeks. The solution is for you and your planner to anticipate your needs and order early.

Most professional bookstore planning firms have astute store fixture buyers on their staff. They have no qualms about exploring every avenue to search out good, reliable manufacturers or sources of equipment and accessories which are just right for your bookstore.

CHAPTER 7

LIGHTING ELEMENTS AND COMMUNICATION SYSTEMS

WHEN WE ARE STRUCK by the ambiance of a bookstore, it is the total visual effect that sharpens our senses and raises our feeling of expectation. We do not visually isolate the type of lighting, books, merchandise, or their arrangement. We see all the interior elements of the bookstore as a single element, a total picture. It is the contrast between unintrusive light falling on the inventory, the color, form, and textures of the background, and the source and angle at which light is delivered that creates the picture. The total effect is aided by the design of the lighting, never overstated or unwelcoming. The quality and maintenance of a store's lighting will make all the difference between a conventional bookstore and an extraordinary one.

It is essential for adequate light to be delivered to the proper location in a bookstore. Lighting is needed to create visibility for customers to circulate and locate book titles and other articles of merchandise. There must be enough visibility inside the selling space for customers to make selections comfortably, inspect the merchandise, and verify its content and quality. The ideal solution for both good visibility and comfortable browsing is to augment general illumination with sufficient accent lighting. The imaginative use of accent lighting can have a significant impact on the interior. It is needed in generous amounts to attract customers into remote areas of the bookstore and to direct their attention to specific promotional displays and major signs, announcing the key departments.

MERCHANDISING WITH LIGHT

The principal contribution of lighting in a bookstore is to stimulate the sale of books and merchandise. Lighting contributes to a successful sale in three ways: by giving customers a good first impression of the sales space, by creating in them a desire to buy, and by helping them evaluate their selections. The design of the entire sales space—from traffic plan and departmental organization to the selection of materials, colors, and textures for walls, floors, and ceilings—will be vitally influenced by the lighting design. No engineering rule requires the ceiling lighting pattern to be the same throughout the store. Rigid, overall uniformity of sales floor lighting is not only monotonous but out of character with the first objective of bookstore lighting—the promotion of book sales.

Light is used to set the stage for browsing and shopping. With a skillful lighting design, the store planner and designer can accomplish as much to create the char-

The lighting fixtures and the type of lighting selected establish the ambiance of the bookstore.

Barnes & Noble, 18th Street & Fifth Avenue, N.Y.C. (Photo: Ken White)

HID lighting, Minnesota Book Center *(Photo: Ken White)*

Incandescent pendants and fluorescent tubes, Barnes & Noble Sale Annex, 18th Street and Fifth Ave., New York *(Photo: Ken White)*

Cold cathode cove lighting Rizzoli/Atlanta *(Photo: Ken White)*

acter of a bookstore as with any other element, and can also provide the means to easily vary it week to week.

General illumination is used for visibility and atmospheric effect. It is a good rule to light books and merchandise two to three times more brightly than their surroundings in order that they may attract and hold customers' attention. It is good store design practice to emphasize the placement of ceiling light on the merchandise (not on the aisles) and to highlight the feature floor displays with intense illumination. Merchandising with light is important. It must be done correctly and not left to chance.

Square, recessed lighting fixtures, Parkland College Bookstore, Champagne, Ill.

Planning Assumptions

The question facing the bookseller is, "How can I make light work best in my bookstore?" There is no one answer, but for purposes of discussion let us assume that an overall level of 50 footcandles of light, calculated at table height—3 feet above the floor—will suffice for the main sales area. Let us next assume that the problem is to design the lighting system for a new bookstore, or one to be remodeled.

Our first concern will be with the type of light source and where it will be located. Most state electrical codes and most landlords now require that the combined lighting *and* power consumption in new and remodeled retail bookstores not exceed 6 watts per square foot. These constraints have a strong influence on the design of interior lighting for book and general retail stores.

Lighting Flexibility

Bookstores which sell sidelines, and certainly all larger stores, have come to realize that no one lighting solution can satisfy the varied sales and display problems of the entire bookstore. Book jackets and other types of merchandise vary widely in their size, color, and texture from sales department to sales department. Even though the difference may be small or subtle, each sales department has specific lighting requirements. A stationery and supply department, for example, has less need for accent and highlighting than a gift, glassware, or card department.

New lighting requirements have a way of continually turning up in active bookstores. This dramatizes the fact that bookstore lighting plans need to provide just as much flexibility as the store fixture plan. This need comes to the foreground when sales departments are shifted or relocated.

TYPES OF LIGHT

Today there is a wide array of new incandescent, fluorescent, and high-energy discharge (HID) lighting sources with which to create the best and most imaginative lighting in bookstores.

Because some lighting sources deliver more light for the same amount of electricity consumed, selecting the proper system and the proper luminaries (lighting fixtures) can have a significant impact on the amount of electricity required to create the mood and atmosphere we are striving to produce.

The light output of various incandescent lighting sources ranges from incandescent candelabra lamps (bulbs) with less than 8 lumens (light) per watt (power) to high-pressure—HID—sodium lamps which blast out as much as 85 lumens of gold-colored light per watt. The large number of design and power-saving alternatives available to the bookseller makes the selection of the specific lighting source one to be approached with the utmost care.

Light is produced in incandescent lamps by electricity heating a tungsten filament in a vacuum tube until it glows. Similarly, light is produced in a fluorescent tube by using an electrical charge to produce a gaseous discharge which in turn causes the phosphorus coating on the inside of the tube to emit light. HID lamps produce light as a result of an electrical discharge (arc) between two electrodes contained in a quartz tube sealed within an outer glass tube. Metal halide HID lamps utilize certain metal additives in combination with the mercury in the arc tube to produce an extraordinary number of lumens. Both fluorescent and HID lamps require ballasts.

Color Rendition

Each incandescent, fluorescent, and HID lighting source produces light of a different color and temperature. When we say that a light source has a "good color rendition," we mean that the light brings a nearly true color value to the merchandise, environment, and the people on which it falls in the bookstore.

Color rendition is the primary characteristic that makes incandescent lighting so desirable for retailing use. And, as we have seen, a variety of incandescent lamps are available for use in bookstore lighting systems. Incandescent lamps bring out warm red, orange, and yellow tones, and the quality of the light is usually soft and flattering. But the combined costs of electrical power and heat generated by the lamps, which in turn escalate air conditioning cost, are the main disadvantages of incandescent lighting systems.

Fluorescent tube lamps have been the most popular light source used in bookstore lighting systems for several decades. Fluorescent luminaries most commonly seen in bookstores are rectangular in shape, 2 feet wide, 4 feet long, and generally recessed into modular ceilings. However, smaller 2-foot-square shapes are becoming increasingly popular. These small, unobtrusive luminaries use several U-shaped fluorescent tubes as their light source. Straight fluorescent tubes are available in many sizes, from 5¼ inches up to 8 feet, and in diameters from ½ inch up to 2⅛ inches. They are available in a large range of colors, in different intensities, and are classified as standard, high output, and very high output.

EXHIBIT 7.1

COMPARISON OF LIGHTING SOURCES USED BY TYPES OF BOOKSTORES

Type of Bookstore	LIGHTING FIXTURE TYPE					Decorative graphic lighting
	Fluorescent	Incandescent	HID	Track	Chandeliers	
Discount	1x8 Surface exposed tubes	No	Surface downlight	Exposed	No	Yes
Chain	2x4 Recessed	No	No	No	No	Yes
College and general	2x4 Recessed	Circular Recessed	Surface downlight and indirect	Exposed	Complementary style	Yes
Specialty	2x2 Recessed	Square and circular recessed	No		Recessed	Complementary style	Yes
Quality	2x2 Recessed	Square and circular recessed	No		Recessed	Complementary style	Yes

*As required by local code.

There are numerous names for fluorescent lighting tubes. Warm white tubes produce a quality of light that is closest to incandescent light, accentuating warm tones. The color temperature of the light fluorescent tubes produce can have a sanitizing effect on wood finishes, merchandise, and book jackets. Even the warm white fluorescent light will soak up the color red—for example, in red oak—and turn the warm red wood color to a honey tone, when that wood surface is directly illuminated by the warm white fluorescent light.

Metal halide lamps generate a quantity of light, the color rendition of which is somewhere between incandescent and warm white fluorescent light. This desirable feature, combined with the efficiency and economy of HID lighting, makes it the most desirable new system to use for the general lighting of sales areas. It also accounts for the increased popularity of HID lighting in bookstores.

LIGHTING THE BOOKSTORE

The most successful lighting design solutions are not contrived. They are flexible and adaptive to the variety of display lighting situations which take place in the store. The *extent* of feature lighting is determined by the physical size of the sales and display area. The *flexibility* of the system is controlled by how well the main ceiling lighting sources are coordinated and integrated with the merchandise layout. The *effectiveness* of the lighting system is determined by how well the system is maintained. The *relationship* of the various lighting sources is shown on the following page.

There are several unique problems involved in designing the lighting of bookstores. Illuminating the perimeter walls is the primary one. For bookstores with low ceilings—from 7 feet, 6 inches, to 10 feet—the choice of a continuous band of fluorescent light mounted in a cornice or valance at the top of the wall selling fixture is a good solution. For a long, narrow shop, a single strip of fluorescent light is sufficient, though. In shops with large sales areas, a double row of staggered

Wall Wash	Light Cornice	Emergency*	Exit*	Nightlight*	Decorative Graphic Lighting
No	Yes	Yes	Yes	Yes	Yes
No	Yes	Yes	Yes	Yes	Yes
Occasionally	Yes	Yes	Yes	Yes	Yes
Yes	Yes	Yes	Yes	Occasionally	Yes
Yes	Occasionally	Yes	Yes	Occasionally	Yes

fluorescent lighting is necessary. The stagger strip has the advantage of lapping one tube over the other at the joints where the tubes meet. This "lapping" eliminates dark spots and the "wall scalloping effect," caused by space between the lamps, seen in so many bookstores.

If, on the other hand, book stacks and display fixtures extend up to the ceiling, lighting the upper perimeter wall is a second challenge. Several design options which may be used to overcome this problem are:

1) Placement of ceiling luminaires close enough to the wall fixture to illuminate vertical fixture surfaces and merchandise

2) Construction of a recessed light pocket in the ceiling with strips of fluorescent or cold cathode (neon) light to illuminate the wall and merchandise

Lighting Sources. (1) Strip fluorescent light in light pocket; (2) strip fluorescent cornice light; (3) recesed incandescent light; (4) surface-mounted track light (5) recessed 2 × 2 fluorescent light; (6) recessed incandescent wall washer.

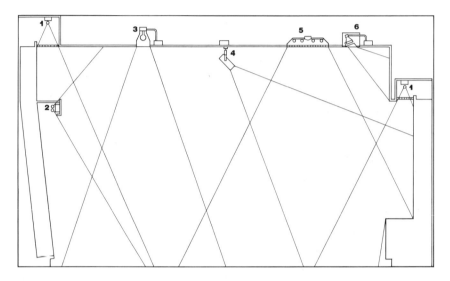

Strip recessed fluorescent lighting, Georgia Tech Bookstore, Atlanta, Ga. *(Photo: Freeman Payne)*

Rizzoli/Georgetown *(Photo: Ken White; architect, Fillipo Perego, Milan, Italy)*

EXHIBIT 7.2

Type of store	Valance	Ceiling
Mass market	1 Fluorescent tube	General lighting
Sale books	1 Fluorescent tube	General lighting
Small general	2 Fluorescent tubes	General lighting
Large general	2 Fluorescent tubes	Ceiling-mounted tube
Small specialty	2 Fluorescent tubes	Recessed trough
Hi tech specialty	Track light	General illumination
College	1 or 2 Fluorescent tubes	General lighting
Museum	Wall washer	Recessed trough
Chain	1 Fluorescent tube	General lighting

3) The suspension of a continuous tube lighting fixture from the ceiling, parallel to the high wall fixtures, to light the surface

There is also the alternative of employing a system of ceiling-mounted wall washer luminaires framing projectors, or track lighting. I have used each of these systems and found that each contributed significantly to the mood I sought to instill. Listed below are examples of how some of these alternatives may be used.

Lighting Show Windows

The principles that apply to interior lighting should also be observed in treating show window areas:

1. The source of light or its reflected glare should be unobtrusive.

2. The light must never be allowed to shine into the customers' eyes. High wattage in window lighting can help keep reflections to a minimum.

3. The use of spotlights, not floodlight bulbs, on highlight displays as well as general merchandise presentations. Spotlights add a feeling of excitement and textures while breaking up the flatness of a window or department or display area.

4. Spotlights must be focused on the top half of mannequins and forms and on the center area of all other pyramids and merchandise groupings.

Track lighting, as discussed below, offers one of the most creative ways to adapt these principles to retail bookstores.

Track Lighting

Incandescent light track systems have the flexibility of permitting a wide variety of fixture heads to be placed anywhere along their lengths. Light tracks are commercially available in 2-, 4-, and 8-foot lengths, made in single and three-circuit varieties, with power saving and flexibility advantages discussed later in the chapter.

Fittings are available which allow tracks to be turned 45 and 90 degrees and to be directly mounted, vertically, or horizontally, on walls and ceilings.

Tracks should be located over main aisles and be parallel to perimeter walls for most effective light angling and distribution. The general rule for placement of light tracks to illuminate the upper one-third of the wall in bookstores with 10-foot-high ceilings is: Place the track a distance of 30 inches from the wall. This will create a suitable 45-degree angle for the track light fixture. If space limitations make it necessary to depart from this rule of thumb, move to the far side. A fixture with hinged barn doors, a theatrical screening device, can be used to screen off most of the side glare.

Contract Design Center Bookstore, Chicago (*Photo: Ken White*)

Once the decision is made to use track lighting to illuminate books or merchandise near a reflective surface such as a mirror, or in a show window, keep the track as close to the mirror or window as possible. If it is not feasible to locate the tracks closely enough, position the track vertically or at the floor so that any stray light or reflections can only be seen from a point in the space that is rarely frequented, i.e., one where there is little traffic. Glare can be reduced by illuminating the merchandise objects directly overhead or at a very oblique angle.

Multiple-Circuit Tracks   The advantage of three-circuit tracks is their capability to control the lighting and conserve energy. The number of track light heads one may hook onto a track is dependent upon electrical load (total wattage of fixtures being used) and special circuit switching and/or dimming requirements assigned to the track. Major tracks should be wired with at least two circuits. This will permit some lights to be turned off while others remain on, or are dimmed at off hours, or when sunlight is flooding the store area where the lights are installed.

Track Lighting for Soft Goods   Illuminated track lights can provide faceout displays with the additional impact and punch needed to point up merchandise and create drama and excitement. As we have seen, 30 degrees from vertical is the recommended strike angle on walls; it is also the recommended strike angle for free-standing merchandise displays. The 30-degree angle will ensure that the front of the merchandise—not just the top—is lit, and that is singularly important.

Track Lighting for Show Windows   As with its other systems, the character of the bookstore will determine the type of lighting installation best suited for its show window. A popular price store which features stock massed in large quantities may be illuminated by vertical and horizontal strips of fluorescent lights, sometimes covered with plastic sleeves, to create unusual color and shadow effects.

Better specialty bookstores use a window ceiling light track installation onto which decorative and directional incandescent light fixtures of high wattage are installed. There may also be a shielded source of fluorescent light recessed in the ceiling and directed downward to the floor at the back or side walls of the show window.

Accessories for the lighting installation are an essential part of good window display. When colored light is wanted to dramatize a particular theme display, inexpensive snap-on gelatin filters may be attached to most track lighting fixtures to produce colored lighting effects. Standard, inexpensive, clear incandescent lamps can be used with these filters to produce a full spectrum of color effects. With these lamps one avoids the use of energy-consuming colored lamps.

Lamps with these colored filters can be carefully directed to wash the window background (if there is one) with color. When focused on merchandise, colored light should intensify or dramatize the product color, not distort it. A pink light on a bouquet of roses or red jackets is fine, but it should not spill over onto a display of green bound books or giftware.

For a discussion of other aspects of lighting, see Chapter 9, "Signage and Graphic Systems."

OTHER ELEMENTS OF THE LIGHTING SYSTEM

Time Clocks

Time clocks are simple control devices designed to automatically switch exterior sign, show window, and other designated lighting on and off at prescheduled times. Most small bookshops require only one or two of these inexpensive devices, but larger stores with show windows on two, three, or four sides of their perimeter require many more. When three-circuit lighting tracks are employed in the windows, installation becomes more involved. In this situation, one time clock is used to control each circuit. In large window installations, time clocks trigger delays which in turn activate contactors—large-capacity switches—that actually turn large batteries of lighting fixtures on and off.

Store planners have found other uses for time clocks and their companions, timer switches. Some store planners use 12-hour timer switches to control rest room, storage area, office, lounge, and receiving dock lighting. Time clocks and timer switches work to the benefit of the bookseller because they are reliable. They remember when to work, and they execute their task of switching on schedule.

Photocells, Switches, and Dimmers

Photocells are small electronic switch control devices sensitive to daylight. These low-cost control devices designed to respond to daylight are often located in show windows and on exterior signs and lighting standards. In operation, the photocell activates a relay (switch), which turns on the light fixture it controls. As the sun rises and daylight becomes brighter, sun rays, striking a sensing device, activate the relay that switches the lighting fixtures it controls—off.

Time clocks and photocells can be designed to work together in the same lighting system. This control combination automatically turns on sign and show window lights on dull, rainy, and blustery days. It also turns the same lights off on bright, sunny days.

Once inside the store, we have several interesting ways to control the lighting effects and power consumption of the lighting system with a flick of a switch, or a twist of a knob. Hi-lo switches with two settings, similar to three-way lamp switches, can be used effectively to control areas lighted with incandescent lamps. This will allow the area to be lighted with softer or brighter settings.

The popularity of dimming controls and switches with booksellers comes from their ability to:

1. Control the balance of the mix of light more easily.

2. Reduce wattage consumption.

3. Extend the life of the lamps.

4. Be readily available and easily installed to control incandescent lights.

Dimmers and hi-lo switches are available for fluorescent lights with special ballasts. Their use, however, is not widespread, as their cost-effectiveness is difficult to justify.

Panel Board Switches

"Where do you want the switches located, and how do you want the lights switched?" are two of the questions most frequently asked of a bookseller planning a new store. The best solution for a small single-floor bookstore is to switch all the lighting and power circuits from a single panel board, which would be located on a clear aisle in the receiving room at the rear of the store. One circuit should be wired to a three-way switch, located just inside the front or rear door. This switch is used to control a single fixture or row of night lights. This lighting is necessary for employees to see and safely find their way in and out of the bookstore after hours. Similar switching arrangements are essential to illuminate stairs to and from basements, balconies, and upper floors.

In multiple-floor stores, it is good practice to locate the main panel and board on the ground floor receiving room and add a secondary panel on each operational level of the bookstore. In large establishments, we would likely have secondary

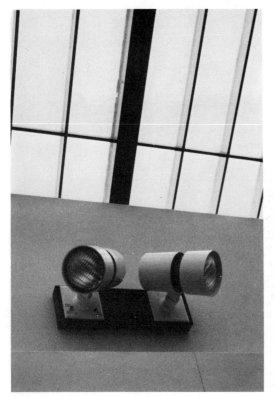

Emergency lighting, University of Connecticut Co-op *(Photo: Ken White)*

Video surveillance cameras, University of Connecticut Co-op *(Photo: Ken White)*

panels to control conveyors, air conditioning, elevators, escalators, and other heavy equipment. There would also be panels for cash registers and power outlets. It is good practice to leave four to six spare circuits open (unused) to accommodate future electrical requirements.

There is no fixed answer to the question, "How do you want the light switched?" The best idea is to alternately switch the light fixtures on separate circuits. This will provide the bookseller with the capability of lighting every other fixture. Switching the lighting fixtures should be arranged in banks or groupings which add up to a total of 1,200 watts on each switched circuit. Incandescent and fluorescent lighting should not be wired on the same circuit.

Twenty-Four-Hour Lighting

In some bookstore situations, it is important to provide 24-hour lighting circuits. These are lights maintained to keep certain areas of the store illuminated for either merchandising or security reasons. In the area of security, the purpose of these lights is to make it possible to observe the presence of unauthorized persons in the store after hours. Twenty-four-hour merchandising lighting occurs in some hotel lobbies, casinos, and airline terminal bookstores. Switches in the power board for the 24-hour circuits are usually painted a bright color and "tied" down to prevent their being accidentally switched off.

Emergency and Exit Lighting

Many local safety codes require bookstores to provide battery-powered emergency lighting equipment which will automatically turn on if there is an interruption in electrical service and the main store lighting fails. The newer versions of these lighting fixtures are neat and unobtrusive. Some models have remote heads. This feature allows the bulk (battery portion) of the unit to be concealed in a convenient place above the ceiling, and only the attractive, adjustable fixture head is exposed. The emergency light must always be aimed at clear aisles leading to an exit to the exterior.

Each exit must be clearly identified with an approved lighted exit sign. These signs are available in a range of sizes, styles, and finishes.

COMMUNICATION SYSTEMS

As bookstores become larger and more complex, the need and extent of internal and external communication systems become more apparent. There is some evidence that booksellers have not given the proper weight to the importance of planning and maintaining effective communication systems. The meaning of the term "communications" has been expanded to the point where today it includes internal and external electronic communication systems, special telephone lines, and devices.

Some of the types of communication systems are:

- INTERNAL STORE COMMUNICATION
  Music and public address systems
  Extension telephones
  Intercom telephones
  Video point of purchase displays

- EXTERNAL STORE COMMUNICATION
  Public (pay) telephones
  Private (unlisted) lines
  Listed telephone lines
  Telex lines

- SPECIAL TELEPHONE DEVICES
  Automatic dialing
  Automatic answering
  Call directors
  Conference calling

- COMPUTER SYSTEMS
  Central processing unit to terminals
  Central processing unit to cash registers
  Store to computer center or service bureau

- SECURITY SYSTEMS
  Burglary and intrusion alarm systems
  Smoke, fire, and sprinkler alarms
  Electronic surveillance systems

Video surveillance control panels, University of Connecticut Co-op *(Photo: Ken White)*

Telephones, Computers, Telex, and Power Outlets

The bookseller will also be asked, "What type of electrical outlets do you need, and where do you want them?" Electrical power outlets are needed in bookstores to activate cash registers, microfiche units, electronic surveillance and alarm systems, business machines, cleaning appliances, television and sound systems, water coolers, dumbwaiters, door and window shutters, weighing scales, computers, clocks, and telex telephones. There are, in addition, a host of other various gadgets, from shrink-wrap ovens and imprint machines to gummed label removers, which require electrical power.

Establishing the proper location for power outlets is important. A considerable number of these costly outlets wind up buried behind store fixtures. It is essential that everyone be aware that the wall outlets, which occur in the wall store fixture runs, must be extended from the wall, through the store fixture base, and mounted horizontally. Power outlets for telephone systems are typically mounted 48 inches above the floor adjacent to the telephone terminal panel. Power outlets—also known as duplex convenience receptacles—are usually located in the lower section of cash wraps and above receiving and marking tables.

Telephones and Buzzers

Telephones to be located on desk tops are simple to locate, but wall telephones should be mounted 60 inches above the floor. Receiving door buzzer push buttons are usually placed adjacent to the door 42 inches above the floor. In small stores, the buzzer itself should be located on the inside of the light cornice board at the rear of the sales area. This will enable the bookseller, who may be alone in the store and working in front, to hear the sound. It will also be heard by anyone working in the receiving room. Larger stores centralize the buzzer in the receiving room.

VIDEO SURVEILLANCE—CAMERAS AND MONITORS

The technological explosion and miniaturization of the past decade has produced compact systems which can be of great value to all booksellers. The decision to include any of these systems in the store, however, must be based on need and the use the individual system is intended to fulfill.

CHAPTER 8

COLOR ELEMENTS AND SCHEMES

COLOR IS AN IMPORTANT ELEMENT in visual merchandising. Color values and color compositions are used to accent and identify books and merchandise on display in the bookstore, to establish the visual proportions of the sales space, and to create the psychological character of the store front and interior selling area. Color is the element which contributes most to a sense of visual unity in a bookstore interior.

COLOR IN MERCHANDISING

More adventurousness on the part of booksellers and planners alike has given some bookstore color schemes a richness and style that are different from the predominance of lackluster bookstores, and this trend will unquestionably continue.

As with every other aspect of bookselling, successful color coordination depends on careful planning and professional know-how.

To successfully accent merchandise, background colors should be either quiet and in harmony with stronger merchandise colors, or else strong in intensity to bring out weaker merchandise color values. An example would be the use of a warm beige background for a cookbook section. Deep chocolate brown or navy blue as the background for a stationery and supply department will emphasize the display of predominantly white papeteries.

Thus, the color, texture, and finish of each exposed building material, graphic element, and store fixture must be selected, coordinated, and specified to harmonize with the merchandising strategy, image, and design of the bookstore.

Color Selection

It is the planner's job to select and coordinate colors, finishes, and color schemes which are in harmony with the design character and image of the client's new bookstore. A color scheme that harmonizes throughout a shop or department provides an integrated visual experience and a comfortable feeling. A bookstore in which every department is a completely different color entity is one with a jumpy feeling. An integrated color scheme is needed to tie together all the departments and visual elements in an overall composition.

In the choice of color, a great deal depends on the bookstore's setting. Bookstores located inside an arcade-enclosed mall or a student union building may require more intense, dramatic color schemes. Bookstores in these settings depend on artificial illumination (which can be controlled), and this influences the selection of color schemes. Artificial light often plays odd tricks with colors. Specialty bookshops or departments—such as historical, children's, mystery, design, or science fic-

Stimulating color schemes that alternate between light and dark, dull and bright, matt and reflective values and surfaces are best for bookselling.

The University Book Store, Madison, WI
(Photo: Ken White)

tion—which are artificially lit can easily afford more dramatic finishes and color schemes, because they are expected by their customers, who enjoy these special effects.

Bookstores with large window areas facing the exterior have another problem (and blessing)—sunlight! The exposure of the major glass areas makes a critical impact on the interior color selection and application. The possibility and extent of color distortions and reflections on books and merchandise caused by sunlight during certain daylight hours must be taken into account and reckoned with.

You won't want a cold blue, green, or violet in a shop with windows facing north; and you won't want an intense red-orange or yellow in one that faces west. If the bookstore is flooded with sunshine through show windows or a skylight part of the day, a bright, high-intensity color scheme would be distracting. On the other hand, if a bookstore faces north, you want colors that are warm, cheerful, and stimulating; colors which create a sense of intimacy.

Using Color to Compensate for Scale and Proportion

When the scale and proportion of the sales space are finally evaluated and understood, colors and finishes are easily selected. Here are several ideas to keep in mind when selecting building colors.

- If a shop is big and barny, darker-toned walls will tend to make the size of the room seem smaller and more friendly.
- Greater visual depth in a department can be planned and accomplished by painting one wall a bright, warm color and three walls a lighter color.
- Colors expand because they reflect light, and make objects seem larger, more spacious, and cheerful.
- Bookstore ceilings are often painted the same color (beige or white) as the walls when they are painted, but height can be added to the ceiling by painting it a lighter color than the walls.
- To achieve a balanced color perspective, a general rule is to paint ceilings three shades lighter than wall colors.
- In a very small, low-ceilinged room, a dark ceiling sometimes works out well. Painting the ceiling a darker value tends to make it disappear.

All kinds of illusions can be produced by the imaginative use of color, but these things are tricky and should be left in the hands of a store planner with considerable knowledge in the use of color.

CONCEPTUALIZING COLOR SCHEMES

Color schemes do not have to be complex to be successful. Most bookstores need surprisingly few colors since so many colors are predetermined—the wood floors and wood store fixtures, for instance, or the natural textures and shades of metal, stone, or masonry building materials. The most successful bookstore color schemes utilize no more than five colors: a neutral floor covering, background walls, the store fixture exterior wood or metal, light cornices, and signage and graphic elements.

One good rule of thumb is to divide the sales areas into the following basic color components:

1. The major color area, or background: floors, walls, and ceiling

2. The secondary color area: the store fixtures and the window treatment

3. The accent color(s): graphics, light cornices and fixtures, occasional furniture, and accessories

Most store planners and designers prefer to keep the background, or major color area, neutral; but colors selected for major color areas can range from among the most neutral to the most brilliant hues, depending upon the size of the area in which they will be used. The secondary area, which includes the wall, center floor, service, and control fixtures and the window treatment, can utilize more intense color combinations. Sharp accent colors are used with discretion in the smallest areas. I find that these unwritten rules generate the most successful schemes and are both safe and useful to follow.

Color Terms

There are numerous good books which deal with the science of color and its theory of application. For our purpose, let us simplify some of the terms which deal with the properties of color and which have been with us for decades.

Color is grouped into three families. A *hue* is a single color in all its lighter and darker variations, such as red, yellow, or blue. Any hue diluted with white is called a *tint*. If, for instance, the primary color yellow is diluted with white, a lighter color, a tint, is the result.

A *shade* is any hue mixed with gray to darken it, except in the case of wood stain. Stains are grayed to begin with. Clear thinner is usually used to lighten them. So we say, "It is a lighter or darker shade of natural wood stain color."

A value of painted or printed color refers to its light or dark color intensity. The intensity of a color refers to the color's purity, that is, the degree of brightness or dullness of a particular color. Another term used for intensity is *chroma*.

By adding gray to any color, its intensity is lowered and it becomes duller. Neutral colors are black, white, and gray; all metallics; and also tints and shades of colors that are predominantly gray or brown in cast, such as beige. Warm colors are red, yellow, and orange. Cool colors are blue, green, and purple or violet.

Colors of light intensity make a small bookstore appear spacious and airy, but to be really interesting they require a contrast of either darker shades, or high intensity. Because neutral shades are compatible with many other accent colors of higher intensity, they are widely used in bookstore color schemes.

The chroma, or intensity, of a color also helps to determine where and how to use it. Strong colors or those of high intensity are best used in small areas, such as graphic panels, and as accent colors. Deep shades of a color can give a book department either richness and warmth or a weighty feeling if they are not relieved by tints.

Stimulating bookstore color schemes that alternate between light and dark, dull and bright, or matte and reflective values and surfaces are usually best for bookselling.

Monotone Color Schemes

One hue—say, khaki—can be employed for an entire store by varying its use on walls, ceilings, or case interiors with materials like paint or vinyl fabric; and by using contrasting textures such as carpet, lacquer, or enamel.

Graphics and Accessory Colors

Signs, graphics, scenic art, paintings, posters, and other nonstructural objects in the bookstore may legitimately "shock" with color. Use of brighter hues for step stools, bookcarts, chair and stool cushions, directories, posters, paintings, signage, smokers, and accent light fixtures is a nice finishing touch to the bookstore and gives the feeling of visual completeness.

TEXTURE

Texture is the description of the surface of a structural or graphic material in its natural state. A texture may also describe the finish of a material, a carved relief or applied decoration, a woven or tufted fabric, or a composite of several of these materials. Textures are usually thought of as dimensional in character, though smooth, etched, sandblasted, and patterned glass mirrors all qualify as textures. Rugged, hammered copper or brass possesses texture as much as do luxurious, mirror-polished brass and copper ceiling tiles.

Moreover, textures are thought of as comfortably rough or smooth, as with natural brick, stone, wood, or plaster surfaces. Textures can be soft, pliable, and elegant with the surface look and feel of suede, rawhide, leather, and fabric. A number of new surface textures in vinyl wall covering and wallpaper, with dimensional texture designs on dull and reflective metallic foil backgrounds, have renewed store planners' interests in these handsome materials.

PUTTING IT ALL TOGETHER

When all the swatches and samples of colors, finishes, and textures of the floor covering, wood, stone, leather, plastic laminate, metal, paint, wallpaper, vinyl, fabric, ceiling, lighting, graphics, and specialty materials have been assembled and agreed upon, they become the color scheme. Smooth color transitions from department to department and from floor to floor are important in achieving a harmonious overall color scheme.

Once determined, the color coordination information is formalized onto typewritten or large hand-lettered color and finish schedules. The color schedules are used to coordinate the bookstore materials, textures, colors, finishes, glass, hardware, and electrical requirements. For convenience and practical use, duplicate samples and swatches of the final selections are glued onto sheets of bristol boards, about 18 inches by 24 inches in size, which instantly become color boards.

Several color boards may be required for a large project and are always necessary in planning multifloor color schemes. With these color boards, one can tell at a glance whether the colors are compatible with the image and character of the bookstore and if they achieve the ambiance desired.

Small duplicate color boards, 8½ inches by 11 inches, are often made to accompany the color specifications and charts, which are bound in ring binders. These are distributed to the project architect and general contractor for coordination purposes.

TIMING AND DISTRIBUTION OF COLOR SCHEDULES

When planning bookstore projects, the timing, preparation, and distribution of the final color and finish information is critical. If at all possible, color decisions should be made during the planning and design stage. Having all the information at hand simplifies the bidding process, expedites the entire building project, and avoids unnecessary delays.

TWENTY COLOR SCHEMES

Twenty color schemes which work are given in Exhibit 8.1. It is important to remember that, in large bookstores, when more than one scheme is used, it will probably contact a main aisle. The aisle color can then be the main color theme which ties the various departmental color schemes together. Colors within each scheme are interchangeable, i.e., the wall color can be used as the store fixture back or the carpet color, and the scheme will still work. When patterned multicolor graphics are to be used, all the colors listed for the five areas in the scheme can be intensified and incorporated.

EXHIBIT 8.1
COLOR SCHEMES FOR BOOKSTORES

Store fixtures	Background walls	Floor covering/ carpet	Ceiling drops, valances or light cornices	Graphics or accents
Oak	Lariat tan	Chestnut brown	Scarlet	White
Walnut	Lemon	Slate	Green and white	Cinnamon, white
Walnut	Cream	Cinnamon	Cream	Black, curry yellow, white
Walnut	Beige	Emerald	Walnut	Bronze, white
Pine	Beige/russet	Russet	Adobe gold/white	Black, adobe gold, white
Walnut	Curry Yellow	Walnut	Yellow and white	Black, brass, white
Beige	Twine	Forest green	Beige and natural	Emerald, bronze, white
Oak	White	Yalta blue-gray	Honey gold	Black, brass, cinnamon
String	Mint green	String	Emerald and white	Gold, emerald, white
Walnut	Cathedral gray	Gray flannel	Bronze gold	White, mint green
Red oak	Mello melon	Edwardian gray	Tangerine	Black, white
White oak	Tomato	Oatmeal	Black and white	Coral, white
Khaki	Lettuce	Khaki	Spring green	Emerald, purple, yellow
String	Slate	Twine	Khaki	Curry yellow, white
Oak	Khaki	Cinnamon	White	Black, orange, white
Oak	White	Black and white	Magenta	Black, red, white
Chestnut	Chestnut brown	Tawny beige	Chinese yellow	Red, orange, white
Walnut	Orange	Edwardian gray	White	Cinnamon brown, curry
Walnut	Blue fox blue	Navy blue	Blue and white	Yellow, coral, white
Cream	Walnut	Daiquiri	Daiquiri	Brass, curry, white

Application of the Color Schemes

Consider the first scheme: natural oak fixtures with tan interiors set against a tan wall on a chestnut brown carpet. Nice, but dreary. Add a scarlet light cornice (accent), display cubes, and white graphics to the tan background—and a beautiful scene emerges!

Let's apply the ninth scheme next. The store fixtures are metal finished in string (gray-beige) enamel set against a mint green wall on a string-colored carpet. The outline of the department is profiled with a clear emerald green Plexiglas valance, which protrudes down from the ceiling 12 inches. The light cornice spanning the wall store fixtures is white. The floor display cubes are gold, emerald, and white. The graphics have white copy on an emerald background.

Too bright? Then look at the fourth scheme. Walnut store fixtures set against beige walls on an emerald carpet, with walnut light cornices and white letters on bronze Plexiglas graphic panels—and you guessed it—Rizzoli International Chicago Bookstore.

What's ahead for bookstore color schemes? My guess is that richer, more vibrant color schemes will continue to emerge in progressive bookstore planning as new, well-designed color trends arrive on the general retail scene.

CHAPTER 9

SIGNAGE AND GRAPHIC SYSTEMS

V ISUALLY SPEAKING, most bookstore graphics are either very expressive esthetically or say virtually nothing. Deciding which is a key first step in bookstore graphic signage and graphic system planning. If you analyze your new bookstore interior and your competition for a few days and your findings are typical, you'll soon discover that most modern bookstore graphic systems are either plain and nondescript, or informative and pleasing.

DESIGN DIRECTION

Choosing which direction to follow is a decision to be made right at the outset. To help you make that important decision, let's analyze each.

The dominant factor underlying virtually every graphic design decision of very plain, nondescript bookstore graphics is "economy." Economy dictates that you limit design to a few signs. Economy also dictates that you specify the cheapest materials, styles, and finishes available, and then secure the lowest bid you can find. Having secured all that, you have virtually ensured that your new bookstore graphic system will be very plain and very nondescript. Inadvertently, your new graphics might very likely tell your customers and potential customers that your bookstore doesn't have much pride in what it is, or what it sells.

Then there's the opposite visual direction—the attractive route—where, for a few dollars more per sign, you add an informative and pleasing look to your bookstore communication system.

Why is this route worth considering? In the first place, there's more to what's communicated in a bookstore sign than the exterior sign message and the bookstore's identity. For instance, at the precise moment an exterior sign is first seen, an impression is made, and a mental image of how and what a bookstore is thought to be begins to materialize.

The image perceived from that first impression affects the customer in two important ways—how he or she immediately responds to the message and whether or not the message is remembered, and if so, in what context. Thus, the more favorable the first impression and the more appropriate the image formed, the more likely the immediate reaction to both the message and bookstore—as well as any subsequent involvement—will be favorable and profitable.

To make the most favorable impression, however, requires a graphic system that's been thoroughly and thoughtfully planned and produced. In particular, its overall visual appearance and order should capture the bookstore's character and personality—professional, practical, friendly, etc. Also, it should reflect visually those traits that best characterize the bookstore's business reputation—dependable, stable, and trustworthy; the book categories or services it sells; who buys them and why. How-

Three-dimensional lettering arranged in an overall, articulated pattern can change a flat, plain wall to a handsome visual statement creating a favorable impression at the entrance.

B. Dalton, 666 Fifth Avenue, N.Y.C.
(Photo: Bill Mitchell)

Design study, Barnes & Noble, Centereach Mall, Long Island, N.Y.

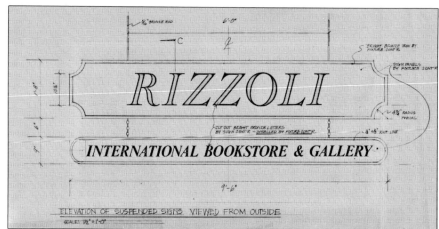

Design detail, Rizzoli Bookstore, Georgetown.

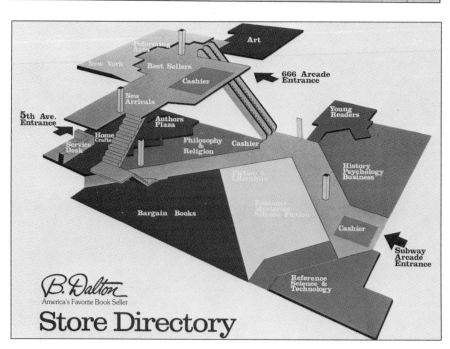

Directory, B. Dalton, 666 Fifth Avenue, New York *(Photo: Bill Mitchell)*

ever, as important as all these factors are, they still don't outweigh the most important factor of all—*your own good taste and preference.*

Signage and graphics for a bookstore should be structured as part of a total identity program which takes into consideration both exterior architectural and interior departmental, category, and directional signage. The basic identification of the bookstore is then extended through its letterhead, envelopes, calling cards, logotypes, and symbols used on store bags and in the advertising of its sales and facilities.

SELECTION OF COLORS FOR GRAPHICS

There are essentially two interior graphic color options used for category, merchandise locations, and information signage. The first option is to introduce an imaginative and eye-appealing graphic system that takes full advantage of contemporary color backgrounds and the latest design and typography concepts. The second option is to use a white background graphic system. Compared with colored sign background, the overall graphics and appearance of white signage are also compelling and impressive, but often more reserved or restrained. Some planners and bookstores, in fact, even consider white sign background stodgy or old-fashioned, out of tune with modernity and the contemporary.

Such opinions are more realistically an expression of personal preference. Surely they don't explain why white signs, shopping bags, and stationery continue to be the most popular choice among bookstore users—by better than two to one.

BRIGHTNESS DIFFERENTIAL

Our ability to distinguish or perceive things is conditioned in large measure by the manner in which objects separate or differentiate themselves from their backgrounds. In bookstore signage, this manifests itself in the difference in contrast between a message and its background.

Each color has a measurable reflectance (see Exhibit 9.1) from which it is possible to calculate the extent to which colors will separate. The greater the separation, the greater the legibility—at least in principle. To qualify as an effective message, the separation or differential should be at least 75 percent. The final choice of which color combination to use is an esthetic judgment. The combination must be the one that will best mirror your bookstore.

If color coding is employed as a device for the purposes of identifying merchandise locations and traffic control, it should be incorporated onto store maps and store directories, and integrated into departmental and category signage.

PLAIN LANGUAGE IN SIGNS

The final purpose of language is to transfer an idea precisely from one mind into another. Thus, the single most important thing to avoid in planning bookstore signage copy is ambiguity.

Ambiguity occurs when:

1. The sign says one thing and obviously means another.

2. The sign contains too many words.

3. The sign obviously makes wrong use of symbols to which we have attached traditional meanings.

In all these cases, the viewer is presented with a situation that may be confusing, distracting, uncomfortable, and possibly dangerous.

EXHIBIT 9.1
BRIGHTNESS DIFFERENTIAL
(In percent)

	Gray	White	Black	Brown	Pink	Purple	Orange	Green	Blue	Yellow	Red	Reflectance
Red	56	80	78	5	66	39	38	10	39	76	0	18%
Yellow	45	18	95	74	28	85	61	73	85	0		74%
Blue	73	88	64	42	79	0	62	45	0			11%
Green	51	78	80	5	62	45	31	0				20%
Orange	29	68	86	34	45	62	0					29%
Purple	73	88	64	42	79	0						11%
Pink	23	41	93	64	0							53%
Brown	54	79	79	0								19%
Black	90	96	0									4%
White	54	0										90%
Gray	0											41%

Legibility and Readability

Legibility is an objective matter concerning the customer's physical ability to see a sign and to distinguish letters or colors. The latter concerns the customer's ability to understand a message once he or she has seen it. Thus, a book category sign could be perfectly legible while at the same time being quite unreadable. This occurs when the message is ambiguous or the layout confusing.

Legibility and the manner in which it governs a planner's choice of letterforms, symbols, colors, and lighting is of primary concern. The way in which legibility is affected by such matters as angular distortion, reflection, location, lighting and distance, layout, and color is equally important.

Legibility-Distance and Letter Size

Legibility-distance is the term used to describe the size a given letter (or pictograph or symbol) must be in order to be seen and comprehended from a given distance, under a given set of conditions or circumstances. Under normal daylight and satisfactory interior lighting conditions, a customer with normal vision can comfortably see capital letters at the rate of 1 inch of height per 50 feet in distance. Thus, a category sign with 1½-inch-high capital letters can normally be read at a distance of 75 feet.

Layout

Proportion, balance, and form are all important in the layout of graphic elements. What we are after is good design and visual communication.

Centering Copy This matter has been the subject of a continuing debate but is chiefly an esthetic consideration. Centering applies mainly to lines that are composed entirely in capital letters. When lines are composed in upper- and lowercase letters, the centered line can look very untidy. This is particularly true when there is a large discrepancy in the length of lines.

Flush Left Copy The modern tendency is to line up sign copy at the left side of the background, or "flush left." The flush right arrangement should only be adopted in special situations as it is always better, from the customer's point of view, to bring the eye back to the same relative position at the beginning of each line.

Vertical Lettering Lettering may be run vertically without serious loss of legibility, providing no more than three lines are displayed together.

Arrow Location There is a tendency to place arrows on messages flush to the left regardless of the direction in which they point. Arrows pointing straight ahead should be placed left or right on the sign, depending upon the location of the sign relative to the subject.

Type Case Selection Should upper- and lowercase letters, or uppercase only, be used?

Both methods are acceptable in bookstores. Messages in upper- and lowercase are some 10 to 20 percent more legible than those set in capital letters only. One major study showed that 90 percent of the people prefer to read upper- and lowercase to capitals. A word set in upper- and lowercase has a more distinctive "word-shape" than the same word set in capitals. The same word set in upper- and lowercase occupies 30 to 35 percent less space than when set in capitals. From the point of view of bookstore category signage layout, uppercase is easier to handle because it forms messages that are conveniently regular in shape.

Fabricated metal letters, Yale Co-op *(Photo: Freeman Payne; architect, Eero Saarinen & Associates)*

University of Connecticut Co-op. Note directional arrow *(Photo: Ken White; architect, Galliher, Schoenhardt & Baier)*

Fabricated plastic letters, University of Connecticut Co-op *(Photo: Ken White; architect, Galliher, Schoenhardt & Baier)*

Yale Co-op *(Photo: Freeman Payne)*

Minnesota Book Center *(Photo: Ken White; architect, Meyers & Bennett)*

TYPES OF SIGNS

Letters, symbols, and backgrounds commonly used in bookstore graphic systems are fabricated from metal, plastic, wood, plaster, pottery, high-pressure laminate, paper, and, of course, cardboard. Individual exterior signs are made of fabricated cast, preformed, molded, or diecut metal, wood, or plastic letters, or are fabricated with metal, plastic, or wood backgrounds.

Interior signs are of several types. Main departmental signs are usually composed with adhesive-backed lettering applied to Plexiglas, wood, or Masonite backgrounds. More elaborate signs are hand-painted. When the copy of a sign repeats itself more than three times, it is usually silk-screened. Carved wood signs are appropriate in special regional situations.

As few as 50 and as many as several hundred signs are needed in a bookstore to categorize and subcategorize book classifications.

Diecut adhesive-backed vinyl film letters are versatile. They can be applied to white or colored strips of cardboard to make these category signs. Letraset—rub-off—transfer letters are also used to create the copy. Category, promotional, and institutional message signs can also be made with a sign machine, a simple device which allows for production of quality signs in small quantities. For more permanent identification and control signs ("Men," "Women," "Authorized Personnel," "Manager"), the copy is usually engraved into high-pressure laminate plaques and attached to doors and wall surfaces with industrial double-face tape.

Flexible Magnets

Because of the high turnover of sign messages in the interiors of most buildings today, flexible and economic sign processes are desirable. The magnetic sign is probably the most widely used. The basis of the magnetic sign is a flexible sheet of magnetic material which serves as the background of the sign. To apply the message, a conventional technique through a piece of paper is used which is laminated to steel foil. It will act as a magnet and have sufficient attraction to iron to hold its own weight.

Decals or transfers are commonly used for credit card information, fire control, alarm, and security signs.

Etching is occasionally used for metal name plaques. Glass etched with a logo, graphic design, or message can be mirrored, creating interesting optical effects.

FINISHES FOR GRAPHIC ELEMENTS

Most graphic elements require some type of finish to protect their material or to achieve a color effect. Lacquer, enamel, and varnish finishes are appropriate for most materials.

Anodizing is a process for applying an oxide coating to aluminum. Several anodizing processes are available which produce a light-colored porous coating that can be dyed in a wide variety of colors. These become part of the metal surface. Many beautiful color combinations can be achieved with this versatile technique.

GRAPHIC LIGHTING

Exterior and interior bookstore signs and panels are usually back-lighted, edge-lighted, face-lighted, or spotlighted. They are made with neon outline letters, individual face-lighted letters, or individual back-lighted letters.

Back-Lighted Signs

Panel signs, letters, and graphic designs are generally lighted from behind through a diffusing sheet of translucent plastic or sandblasted glass. The sign copy is either silhouetted or illuminated in color. Another version of the back-lighted sign now in popular use is one constructed of a metal box with the letters and designs cut out of the metal face. Corresponding letters are cut out of the sheet plastic. These letters are then fastened to the metal face from the inside so that each letter protrudes through the face. The letters and designs are then illuminated by fluorescent lights placed inside the box.

Yale Co-op *(Photo: Freeman Payne)*

Face Lighting

Face-lighted panels are usually recessed with the light source at the top or at the base. The panel is sloped slightly forward so that as much light as possible is thrown onto the face. Where such signs are below eye level, the light source is placed at the top and the panel sloped in the opposite direction. Both forms are only relatively effective when the overall general lighting of the area is low.

Spotlighting

Where a high intensity of light is required on the letter face, spotlights are generally used.

Neon Outline Letters

This is a traditional method of illuminating signs. It consists of running neon tubing around the edge of the letter as closely as practicability and safety considerations will allow. The great advantage of this method, which accounts for its continued popularity, is the fact that it is visible under all daylight conditions and is not confined to nighttime use. It can also be used as a temporary expedient for enlivening an existing sign or fascia. The colors available in neon lighting include plain white, green, dark blue, light blue, ice blue, dark green, light green, blue, jasmine yellow, apricot, rose, amber, flame, magenta, red, and ruby red.

Cut-out wood letters, Louisiana State University Bookstore *(Photo: Ken White)*

Individual Face-Lighted Letters

Face lighting has become the most acceptable method of illuminating individual letters and usually consists of a plastic face with metal or plastic casing inside of which are single or multiple lines of fluorescent tubing. Although its daylight visibility is not as great as that of exposed tubes, it generally has a more distinguished appearance and is almost as effective at night.

Anderson College Bookstore *(Photo: Ken White)*

Individual Back-Lighted Letters

This is a method by which an opaque letter, usually of box construction containing a fluorescent neon tubing, is set away from a reflective surface so that the letter appears black with a halo of light. The area of glow is controlled by the distance which the letter is set away from the wall. This is the least aggressive of the methods of illumination.

All the methods discussed so far are capable of being combined, and their possibilities are limited only by the inventiveness of the planner or graphic signage designer. In addition to the normal types of sign construction, there is a special method of the ultraviolet illumination of fluorescent materials, known as black light, that can give rise to very dramatic effects. It needs closely controlled conditions which are usually possible to achieve in most bookstore environments.

Category signs, Harold P. Smith Bookstore *(Photo: Ken White)*

Specialty Signage

Electromechanical signage is commonly used for news bulletin boards and is usually seen in very high traffic areas. The message can be of a purely temporary nature such as a news item, or the title of a book, or a promotional message, which can be repeated over and over again. Quite a number of firms specialize in the construction of these units, and an obvious use for them is in a CBD bookstore, where their ability to add or change a merchandising message instantly from a central control point, would be valuable.

Video signage: In signage areas which require a constant message turnover, it is desirable in some cases to use a computer-controlled video output device. One can store many thousands of messages in the central computer and these can be displayed at various remote locations throughout the bookstore, using an ordinary television receiving unit.

Audio signage support: Signage messages can become so complex that it may be necessary to reinforce the video part of the sign with an audio backup message

EXHIBIT 9.2
CHECKLIST OF GRAPHIC ELEMENTS

1. BASIC IMAGE

   Creation of symbol
   Design of logo
   Selection of typeface/alphabet to be used
     consistently throughout the bookstore
   Selection of graphic colors

2. GENERAL EXTERIOR BOOKSTORE GRAPHICS

   Architectural signs, sculptured or
     illuminated with:
     Flame
     Flashing and moving lights
     Flood lighting illumination
     Indirect illumination
     Internal illumination
     Neon tube illumination
   Awnings, canopies, and marquees
   Banners
   Permanent window graphics and signage
   Sidewalk showcases
   Temporary (construction) signs
   Movement, time, and temperature devices
   Traffic and directional signs: entrance,
     exit, do not enter, reserved, truck
     entrance

3. MERCHANDISING GRAPHICS AND
   DEPARTMENTAL SIGNS

   Environmental and decorative graphics:
     wallcovering, scenic art, flags and
     banners
   Category signs
   Classification signs
   Subcategories
   Size markers
   Store directory/map: main floor and each
     entrance
   Institutional message signs

   Service desk/service directory
   Portable directories
   Coming events tackboard/chalkboard
   Information
   Cashier
   Theme and promotional signage

4. INTERIOR TRAFFIC AND DIRECTIONAL SIGNAGE

   Room designations (manager, receiving
     room, etc.)
   Elevators/escalators
   Employee lounge
   Rest rooms
   No admittance
   Watch your step
   Exit
   Fire extinguishers
   Fire alarm
   No smoking

5. PRINTING AND STATIONERY

   Office stationery: local, air mail, and
     memo
   Calling cards
   Labels
   Bookmarks
   Store bags—plastic/craft
   Brochures/flyers/catalogs
   Store operating forms
   Invitations/announcements
   Gift certificates
   Gift wrapping

6. MISCELLANEOUS

   Customer totebags
   Employee ID tags
   Employee vests, jackets, smocks

to make sure that people understand it and to give additional reinforcement to the video portion of the sign.

STATIONERY, WRAPPINGS, AND STORE BAGS

Creating and producing stationery, wrappings, and store bags perfectly tuned to the retail character of your bookstore is truly an exercise in subtleties. Almost without exception, the process requires an awareness of, and concern for, the many subtle differences found in each and every element affecting stationery graphics.

It is important to recognize that subtle differences do exist in the typefaces available, the printing process, and the choice of stationery paper, wrapping paper, and plastic bag selected. Choosing the combination that blends best with the design format adds appreciably to the esthetic impressiveness of business stationery, store image, and, in the case of store bags, advertising and visibility.

Some booksellers think that business correspondence serves only one purpose. They simply carry letters from the sender's to the receiver's mailing room, whereupon those envelopes are opened, the letters removed, and the envelopes discarded in the wastebasket, never to be seen by people who really matter.

Their belief in this process usually prompts these same people to keep stationery and bag costs at the barest minimum. Expressionless stationery conveys a dull image, precisely what most booksellers do not need. All of which means that attractive stationery and store bags are well worth considering. When a letter invites a customer or a potential customer to consider the purchase of books or merchandise, a penny or two is a very small price to pay for the appropriate introduction that well-designed and coordinated stationery provides. That difference isn't a cost. It's an excellent investment with an exceptionally high return.

Visually reflecting the quality of the bookstore in the graphic design of the store bags is also an important ingredient in sustaining the store image.

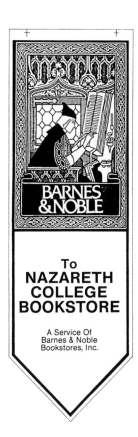

Graphics coordinated with bags and stationery, Nazareth College Bookstore.

CHAPTER 10

GETTING IT ALL TOGETHER

W HEN ALL THE CONCEPTUAL DESIGN elements—store fixtures, floors, walls, ceilings, lighting, colors, and graphics—have been finalized and coordinated with the final preliminary plans, the project schedule and cost estimates should be checked with the building program.

A final project coordination meeting should be scheduled to bring together the bookseller, planner, architect, mechanical consulting engineers, and others who have worked with the plans, to resolve any open questions. This is the time to review models, visual sketches, colors, finishes, and materials and make any final changes. From this point on, changes become both complex and expensive. Assuming that all goes well, the bookseller will instruct the store planner and architect to proceed with preparation of the final plans and specifications.

PROJECT PLANS

In small projects where minor structural or mechanical changes are involved, all the information is usually shown on a single drawing, or, for multifloor projects, on a simple set of drawings and specifications. In larger and more complicated projects, however, separate sets of architectural, structural, and mechanical drawings and indexed specifications are required, covering in detail the work expected and materials required for each division of the work.

Final Coordinating Details

For the large project, the store planner's first step in final planning is to produce final schematic details and schedules of interior floors, ceilings and blocking, lighting and power, partitions, and color finishes. These detail drawings are furnished in sketch form, ready to be drawn and amplified by the project architect, becoming a part of the final contract working drawings and specifications.

Final Building Plans

General architectural and mechanical bookstore building plans normally include details of the arrangement and equipment of elevators, escalators, dumbwaiters, and the back room services. Except in small bookstore projects, separate plans and large ¾-, 1-, and 1½-inch-scale details of the technical and mechanical areas of the bookstore are drawn. Typically, this will include the loading dock; conveyors; receiving, marking, and shipping room; the trash room; accounting and administrative offices; employee facilities; raised galleries; and floor offices. The detail drawings supplement the ⅛-inch or ¼-inch-scale floor plans. The final bookstore fixture plan, arrangement,

The completion of a bookstore project requires the attention of everyone concerned to make sure that loose ends are taken care of and the opening is on schedule.

B. Dalton, 666 Fifth Avenue, N.Y.C.
(Photo: Bill Mitchell)

and equipment details are not included on these documents but are a complete, separate set of drawings.

Fixture Working Drawings

In the case of a small one-floor bookstore, the entire book sales area plan, elevations, and details can be shown on a single drawing. For larger and multilevel bookstores, the layout must be shown floor by floor in a larger set of plans. In the case of very complicated, large store plans, it is a good idea to have a "key overall Plan" drawn at ⅛-inch scale and separate larger (¼-inch) scale plans of segments of the selling floor. These in turn are keyed to the smaller plan. Large drawings are unwieldly and difficult for everyone to handle. I once made a ¼-inch-scale floor plan for the Harvard Co-op—MIT Bookstore, which measured 36 inches high and 60 inches wide; it was very accurate but a "bear" for everyone to work with.

A separate plan should be made for the store fixtures, graphics, sales floor furniture (which includes stools, ladders, browsing tables, and chairs), office furniture, color schemes, equipment lighting, and floor covering. That is, of course, unless one or more of these items is included in the general building construction plans. Each store fixture, piece of furniture, and graphic item should be coded and numbered on the plans for pricing, coordination, installation, merchandising, and reference purposes.

Fixture Specifications

Specifications are clearly written technical descriptions of the work to be performed, material to be used, and services to be rendered to furnish you with the quality bookstore which you have contracted for. They should be carefully read and understood by you. Bookstore plans and specifications must be professional and complete in every respect. Fixture contractors will only execute what is indicated and described. The specifications describe what you should expect of the fixture contractor and stipulate what is expected of him.

Fixture Manufacturers

There are numerous store fixture manufacturers—also known as fixture contractors—who are equipped to fabricate, deliver, and install complete bookstore installations. Many of the best are members of the National Association of Store Fixture Manufacturers, which will gladly furnish you with a list of their members.

The fixture firm's ability to schedule and hold to agreed production schedules and bring together the qualified shop and field installation teams to successfully complete your project is of the utmost importance. Through the field superintendent, the fixture contractor must provide constant supervision and coordination with other building trades during the installation phase. The fixture contractor must usually deliver in a short period of time a complete system of store fixtures that meet with the detailed specifications on which the bid was based and the contract awarded. Because equipping and setting up of a bookstore are so specialized and so demanding, it is best to work with store fixture manufacturers who are experienced with working in a bookstore environment.

The Fixture Contractor Bid List

The fixture contractor invited to bid or negotiate a contract to fabricate your new equipment should be financially sound. Over the years, some fixture contractors have gone out of business in the middle of several projects, leaving clients high and dry. In that situation, the impact on a bookseller can be catastrophic.

When assembling a list of potential bidders for your bookstore project, the best idea is to rely on your store planner's recommendations. The size, capability, past performance, bookstore experience, financial standing, and attitude are an indication of the bidder's ability to successfully complete your project on time and on budget.

The Fixture Contractor's Bid   Several sets of final plans and complete specifications with *bid forms* are supplied to each fixture contractor invited to bid on the project. This is to assure that competitive bids are based on identical requirements. Without this safeguard, there is no way to determine whether the firm submitting the lowest bid has plans to substitute materials of an inferior grade, cut corners, or employ a lower quality of workmanship to fabricate your project.

Two to four weeks are required to solicit and receive store fixture quotations. All quotations should be furnished on the bid forms with any exceptions or alternates noted. The store planner will assist you in analyzing the bids.

Awarding the Store Fixture Contract   All small and most large bookstore fixture contracts are awarded to a single supplier. The potential of a larger contract creates a better bidding-pricing atmosphere, and usually results in a better overall price.

There are, of course, occasions when the size of the project and the date when the store fixtures are needed make it practical and necessary to split the contract. In that event, a contract is usually awarded to one store fixture manufacturer to make and install the perimeter wall fixtures and a second contract to another fixture contractor to make and install the loose and freestanding center of the floor bookselling and service equipment.

Successful fixture contractors should be notified of their selection by the store planner. Selection should be confirmed by a letter of intent from you followed by a contract or purchase order in the agreed amount. Avoid verbal agreements; they lead to misunderstandings. Remember, "Paper does not forget."

Approval of Shop Drawings and Material Samples

Once a contract has been awarded, the planner supplies the successful store fixture contractor with supplementary large-scale detail drawings, samples of color and finish choices, and any other relevant information required to prepare shop drawings and complete the project. In turn, the fixture contractor provides the planner with duplicate sets of several important documents for review and approval. These include the proposed schedule, timed to coincide with the activities of the builder; and a complete set of shop drawings, which illustrates the store fixture contractor's interpretation of the intent of the contract drawings. The shop drawings must indicate proposed materials, finishes, and methods of construction, and any substitutions or changes for evaluation by the store planner. This is to assure that substitutions are equal in quality and that their use will not result in an inferior or shoddy product. The fixture contractor also provides several sets of matched color samples, which are used for quality control and coordination purposes.

When these documents and samples are approved, the fixture production begins. The builder is then given the final color schedules for painting.

CONSTRUCTION AND FABRICATION

The builder (general contractor) now becomes the party responsible for coordinating construction. Equally, the store fixture contractor assumes responsibility for coordinating fabrication and installation of the fixtures. This requires a lot of good, old-fashioned interaction. It is the fixture contractor's responsibility to organize and schedule store fixture production in the plant and to organize installation work at the site to coincide with the agreed-upon planning schedule.

FOLLOW-UP, EXPEDITING, AND SUPERVISION

While the store fixture manufacturer is mainly responsible for maintaining the quality and scheduling of the store fixtures, the store planner closely follows each step. Shop production schedules are generally more reliable than those of general construction. In small and medium projects, a trip to the site from time to time may be sufficient. In large projects, the planner may advise the bookseller that a part- or full-time clerk of the works be hired for near or full-time supervision. The planner should also, as necessary, inspect the bookstore fixtures and fabricated items such as the graphics, etc., at the fixture manufacturer's plant or graphic studios before they are shipped to the new bookstore. Both the bookseller, store planner, and architect must meet with the builder regularly to expedite any decisions, approvals, or other matters that will affect the scheduled progress of the bookstore project throughout the construction period.

Avoid giving any instructions directly to the contractors or their workers. Channeling all instructions affecting the contract or schedule through the store planner and architect will keep communications straight. It will also prevent confusion, possible duplication of work, and expense.

Changes Bookstores built in some new, and virtually every old, building encounter situations which require changes in the construction and store fixture contracts during the progress of the work. Careful planning and complete, professionally prepared drawings and specifications can reduce changes to the minimum. Because bookselling is still more of an emotional art than a science, new merchandising ideas are added or dropped and new departments or services have a way of creeping into most projects. When a change is made, it usually affects the floor, walls, ceiling, lighting, store fixtures, and graphics. Structural changes are more serious and, therefore, more costly. In old buildings, fire or water damage to concealed members must be dealt with, as well as a number of regulatory agencies. For example, one agency might approve an exterior lighted sign and another not. The building inspector's field decision could go either way. So be prepared when some one at some time says, "This will be an extra."

Approval of Payments During and at the end of the project, the planner must certify all payments made by the bookseller to the store fixture manufacturers for completed work as they are submitted. Basically, it is the planner's responsibility to see that the plans and specifications are followed and the bookstore interior built as designed. It is the architect's responsibility to approve the builder's requisitions for payment and see that he complies with the building plans and specifications.

Construction coordination meeting. Author, Bobbie Kroman, and Joe Columbo. *(Photo: Bill Mitchell)*

COMPLETING THE PROJECT

About five weeks before scheduled completion of the job, it is a good idea to get a solid fix on the status of every element of the project—building, interior, exterior, signs, etc. This is the time to break up bottlenecks and verify that fabrication and construction is on schedule. Once an opening date has been set and opening media advertising, publicity, promotional activities, and the personnel and merchandise move-in are scheduled, it is extremely difficult to change dates. Check early and avoid the last three days "to hell with the overtime cost; the store has to open" attitude. This kind of an operating environment is always expensive and can usually be avoided.

Everybody Pitches In

The store planner, architect, builder, fixture, graphics, and other contractors should, in the final days of completion, "come to general quarters" and assist in the expe-

Installing lighting and store fixtures *(Photo: Bill Mitchell)*

Stocking wallcases *(Photo: Bill Mitchell)*

Processing the opening inventory *(Photo: Bill Mitchell)*.

Opening publicity *(Photo: Bill Mitchell)*

Setting up electronic cash registers *(Photo: Bill Mitchell)*

Opening day. Vice President Kay Sexton and Bette Fenton invite guests to sign the register

Guest greets Floyd Hall, center and William Andres, Chairman of the Board, The Dayton Hudson Corp.

A.B.A. Executive Director, G. Roysce Smith (center facing) came to the reception

Open for business (*Photo: Bill Mitchell*)

diting, scheduling, and supervision of every activity necessary to open the bookstore. This can include taking down construction signs and barricades, washing windows, cleaning lighting fixture lenses, removing trash, and, within the contract limits, generally policing the exterior and interior of the bookstore.

To prevent last-minute rushes, the bookstore staff should be receiving, marking, moving, and stocking fixtures while interior construction activity is still underway.

As stock is shelved, store fixtures should be carefully wrapped in plastic to reduce dust, damage, and theft. The store planner should supervise final installation of your special display items, like window etageres, glass cubes, and so forth.

With Thanks and Good Luck—The Store Opens

Then, one day, just as sure as God made little green apples, everything falls into place and your bookstore is ready for its grand opening.

The completed bookstore is the result of the study of the site location and the competition; conceptualizing an effective image; dozens of drawings; hundreds of creative working hours; blood, sweat, and ink; a lot of second and third guessing; and above all, imagination.

Hopefully, this will have proved to be a solid, joyful, and creative experience for you, your staff, the store planner, architect, builder, fixture contractors, and the craftsmen who built the store.

Now, your bookstore is ready to fulfill its primary purpose—to sell books. Good luck!

PART TWO

A PORTFOLIO OF BOOKSTORE PLANS, PHOTOGRAPHS, AND DESIGN SKETCHES

PART ONE OF THIS BOOK examined the manner in which bookstores are planned, designed, and built. Part Two presents a portfolio of plans, photographs, and design sketches of the interior of 22 bookstores. The portfolio visually demonstrates that each bookstore is unique in its own way. There is no single one and only best kind of bookstore, save one—the kind of bookstore that makes people want to read books and buy related articles.

Planning bookstores also includes chance, a quality no amount of determined effort alone is able to achieve. Given certain circumstances and certain touches, the final design will have the effect of being something natural and easily achieved, which is exactly what it wasn't. You can walk into a successful bookshop and experience this effect in its most subtle form.

In this section you will find yourself traveling on a visual journey through plans and illustrations starting in the Northeast, in New York. From there, you will swing across the Midwest to Minnesota, through the Southwest and South, and back up the Atlantic Coast. You will have stopped to look at a cross section of unique bookstores in 12 states, as they appeared when they were built.

These bookstores were chosen from more than 800 projects to appeal to a wide audience of booksellers as well as to a limited one of professional store planners. The bookstores illustrated are not only distinguished for their contribution to the bookselling profession but are representative of their type for planning, merchandising, and interior architecture. If you should visit some of these stores, you will quickly discover they have come a long way from where they began.

When looking at an early bookstore, the important point is not its age, but how vital is its appeal. To keep the appearance of a retail store alive is to keep alive the store itself. For the fact that, in that sense, all the bookstores shown here are vital and alive, applaud the people who own and operate them now; and applaud other bookstores like them which have made their own equally important contribution to the bookselling profession. For, in a few years from now, there will be far too many imaginative bookstores for still another portfolio to contain.

B. DALTON BOOKSELLER

666 FIFTH AVENUE
NEW YORK, N Y

THE FIRST FLOOR of this 25,000-square-foot bookstore faces Fifth Avenue and is enclosed by a glass wall of show windows (1) set behind a row of black granite columns. A huge display of new books, reflected in show window step displays of mirrored chromium, is cantilevered in the front show window over the grand stairway leading down to the main floor (2).

From the outside, the shop is given an appearance of unity by the continuous statuary bronze-colored graphic panels with polished bronze lettering set between the granite columns. Once through the entrances in that wall, the true nature of the shop, that of Dalton's merchandising formula—"nothing but books"—is immediately clear.

The central theme of the design is books, lots of books: books in piles, books in stacks, and books in pyramidal constructions. The artistic unity within the walls is that of purpose—everything devoted to the service of the customer. There are tables, gondolas, steps, endcaps, wallcases, book beams, ladders, and raised galleries, all of which flow in a natural way and divide the space vertically, creating extra visual excitement. Through arches formed by a beam of two rows of books slung between the first rows of columns is a view of the New York Gallery and the Performing Arts Department. Customers on the ramped gallery look down into the Art Department with its elegant floor-to-ceiling bookcases of dark wood filling out the remainder of this first-floor space.

Glass-sided escalators carry patrons to the main display floor below and the departments devoted to philosophy and religion (3); home crafts (4); fiction and literature, romance, mysteries and science fiction, history, psychology, and business (5); reference, science and technology, bargain books (6); and young readers. Some 100,000 titles are stocked in these departments, each color-coded for easy identification, with both hardcover and paperback volumes lined up side by side on the shelves.

The main floor is about the size of two high school gymnasiums. The walls are lined with orderly rows of bookcases bound with a lighted cornice and accessed with rolling, stained oak ladders.

This floor is divided into three selling areas by wide bronze-colored quarry-tiled aisles. Books are visually merchandised on either side of the aisles

4

5

in an angular plan on rich walnut and orange-colored theme tables, step displays, and gondolas that are set at opposing angles on large three-sided areas of oiled oak parquet flooring.

"There is a lot of impulse buying in bookstores. Most people come in looking for a specific title or for a book in a specific area of interest. But the average purchase in a Dalton store is two books—half the time the second book is bought on impulse," Dalton's president, Floyd Hall (7), said. "Remember, when this store is planned, we want people to think of us as the place that will have the books that they want."

There are three carpeted bookselling galleries of varying heights and colors on the main floor, employed as a means of organizing space and creating a sense of discovery within the departments. The walnut paneling and gray-carpeted environment of the north gallery reflect the serious mood of the books displayed there, while appealing to the tastes of a special group of customers. "REFERENCE SCIENCE AND TECHNOLOGY" is spelled out with white serifed letters on the transparent bronze valance outlining the department.

At various times readings and storytelling take place in the Young Readers Department in the appealing west gallery, with its blue-gray and green carpet (8) and accented color scheme.

The south gallery, with its beige walls and burnt orange carpet, is ringed with thousands of beautifully colored and designed books related to cooking, homemaking, and home crafts. It is also the home of the Authors' Plaza. A steady flow of authors and publicists, sometimes as many as 10 or 12 in a single week, come to the Authors' Plaza in the south gallery and stay for a few hours or more (9). The Plaza is sunk two steps down into the gallery, with wide steps that double as seats and display spaces. The Authors' Plaza, a place for autograph parties, cooking demonstrations, lectures, readings, musical happenings, and other scheduled customer-oriented events, was conceived and especially designed for these purposes. It is an entity unto itself with its own unique lighting and sound system, handmade oak table, and comfortable chairs.

The store offices and customer service desk are placed to the east of the Authors' Plaza and raised one step up. The 25-foot-long walnut-faced service desk, where customers transact special business and order out-of-print or foreign books, is in a clear area set apart from heavy traffic lanes.

6

7

8

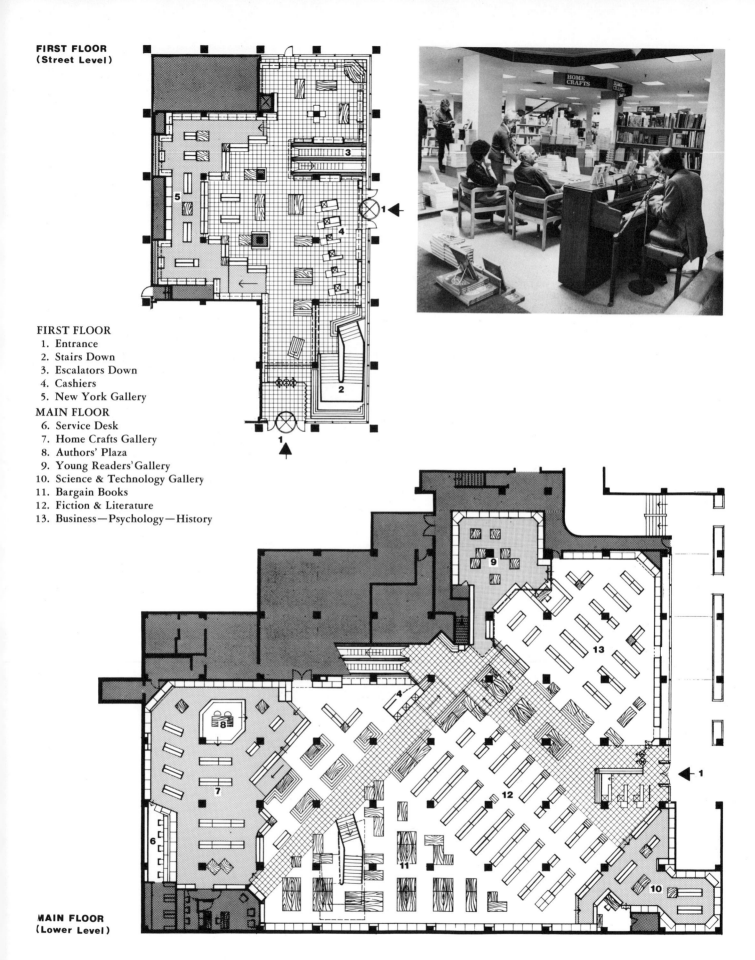

FIRST FLOOR
(Street Level)

FIRST FLOOR
1. Entrance
2. Stairs Down
3. Escalators Down
4. Cashiers
5. New York Gallery

MAIN FLOOR
6. Service Desk
7. Home Crafts Gallery
8. Authors' Plaza
9. Young Readers' Gallery
10. Science & Technology Gallery
11. Bargain Books
12. Fiction & Literature
13. Business—Psychology—History

MAIN FLOOR
(Lower Level)

B. Dalton has an in-house store planning department. It is self-contained and rarely uses outside consultants. However, for the 666 Fifth Avenue project, it broke tradition and went outside the organization to find a bookstore planning consultant.

"This store has been a hell of a planning and construction job for everybody," Jack Ford, Dalton vice president of planning and real estate, said. "Yet it's only one of the 61 stores that we opened in 1978. Had we not opened it, we would have opened 60 new stores. The difference between 60 and 61 is minute, but this store itself probably took the same effort as the other 60 stores combined!"

The million-dollar project was indeed a different one, and it raised the question of why Dalton would open a huge new store on upper Fifth Avenue.

"We really have always felt that New York is such a completely different market and there are so many things that happen first there and faster there—that if we could tap into that with some quick informational feedback, it could really positively affect the other stores," said Dick Fontaine, executive vice president.

Bob Crabb, vice president of merchandising, who coordinated the project for Dalton, explained that in Dalton's view "Manhattan is the center of the publishing industry; there is the potential for enormous sales and there is the opportunity for corporate visibility and the prestige factor of a Fifth Avenue location."

Naturally, one might expect some grand strategy for the New York market. Would the merchandising techniques that proved to be so effective around the country work on Fifth Avenue?

John Schultz, vice president of merchandising, said, "The 'New York Strategy' was really a handy term that sounds as if it means so much more than it really does. The New York strategy is really no different than the strategy that has really built this company," John says. "We simply believe that we can bring not only more books better displayed, but the right books better displayed to more people and a more pleasing shopping environment in New York than anyone else can. That's our strategy. It's pretty simple."

In explaining the visual merchandising appeal of the store, Stan Pressler, vice president of stores, said, "If you walk down one of our aisles, the displays stop you; they magnetize you to the merchandise. I think the average customer does stop and look, which, of course, is essential in any retail business."

Throughout the planning stages, I was reminded that, "One of our strengths, one of the things we keep keying in on is our services. We know how to serve best." Bobbie Kroman (the Dalton manager of Fifth Avenue) hired a very professional crew of people, and Dale Hardman came on board as merchandising manager. Bobbie is very eager to please and very capable and very eager to succeed; and that is being communicated to and demonstrated by the staff that she hired and manages. In the end, it is the staff and the managers who make the customers feel good about shopping in the bookstores we design.

This corporate attitude was nicely bundled up by John Pope, director of advertising, promotion, and publicity, in the store opening advertising. The theme, "New York, you're entitled," was spread across four pages in *The New York Times* and *The Daily News*, and was seen on television and posters on the sides of buses around town on the morning of November 14—opening day.

New Yorkers learned they were entitled . . .

"... To meet B. Dalton, America's favorite book-seller.

... To a great selection of books.

... To friendly personal service.

... To a real bargain.

... To a bookstore that sells nothing but books.

... To a bookstore that's exciting to shop.

... To a great Grand Opening Celebration. Come see B. Dalton today. There will be plenty of excitement all week long." And there was.

1

2

3

BARNES & NOBLE SALES ANNEX

DOWNTOWN—18TH STREET AND 5TH AVENUE
NEW YORK, NY

4

NEW YORKERS SEEM to get most of their news from *The New York Times*, and on Tuesday, October 14, 1975, the *Times* carried an ad across two full pages announcing the new, expanded, absolutely mind-boggling Barnes & Noble Sales Annex to New Yorkers. The ad proclaimed that there has never been anything like it, in bookselling or in any kind of selling.

Barnes & Noble leased space on Fifth Avenue between 17th and 18th Streets, and stocked it with 300,000 books covering almost every conceivable subject. The new space combined with the existing main store, located directly across Fifth Avenue, qualified it to be recognized by *The Guinness Book of World Records* as the most cavernous bookstore in the world. It was the first step in Barnes & Noble's president, Leonard Riggio's dream of turning lower Fifth Avenue into the bookselling center of the world.

The store expanded by stages over the course of several years. Initially, the first floor occupied 40 feet of frontage on Fifth Avenue (1) devoted entirely to a customer parcel check (no packages, boxes, or bags are allowed in the store); an escalator to the second floor (2); promotional sale tables and stacker boxes, laden with remainder books and games; and eight cashier stations, which expand to 10 at Christmas and other busy times.

The second floor contains, as its focal point, 40 feet of bins arranged to stack large quantities of *The New York Times* bestsellers (3). The entire floor is equipped with book sales tables stacked with current general books (4), recent bestsellers, and up and coming titles. Open 7 days a week, the facility is a book lover's paradise. Unlike jumbled sale tables in many stores, where one might have to plow through 15 accounting titles to get to one cookbook, the Sales Annex books are organized and stacked neatly on thousands of feet of shelving and librarylike rimtop tables. The new Sales Annex children's department stocks 100,000 hardcover children's books, with emphasis on books of an educational nature, for just $1.00 each.

But it is the large stacks of remainders, with general categories such as cooking, film and photography, art, sports (5), music, humor, antiques and decorating, sections of foreign language books, engineering and technical books,

5

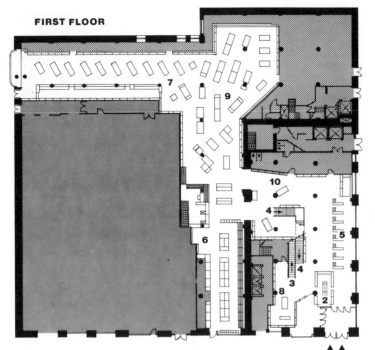

FIRST FLOOR

SECOND FLOOR

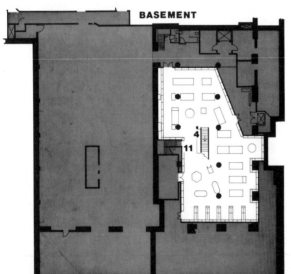

BASEMENT

FIRST FLOOR	BASEMENT
1. Entrance	11. Book Ends
2. Book & Parcel Check	
3. Escalator Up	**SECOND FLOOR**
4. Stairs Up	12. Art
5. Cashiers	13. Photography
6. Classical Records & Tapes	14. *New York Times* Bestseller List
7. Scholarly Books	15. Current Fiction
8. Games	16. Medical & Scientific
9. Children's	17. Paperback Books
10. Discounted Paperback Bestsellers	

6

medical books, dictionaries, encyclopedias, and sets, without a list price to be seen anywhere, which qualify this store to rightfully state that it is one that has never been seen before.

The plan of this store was just as carefully considered and painstakingly arranged as any that was ever planned. The creative concept was entirely Riggio's, but the design director of Barnes & Noble and a project designer from our firm carried the main planning and design burden. From the beginning it was agreed that the design should be "camp"—a blue jean look with rich, deep earth tone colors, rough-sawn natural wood, and one color of carpet, selected to unify the three selling floor spaces of the store.

Eight-foot-long strips of bare fluorescent bulbs were arranged in large rectangles to create a uniform level of light. It produced impressive amounts of light and contributed to the ambiance. The high tech approach to lighting was both stylish and functional. Thick lettered graphics were painted deep yellow and white on natural (dark brown) Masonite.

The store fixturing system is a study in tasteful simplicity. The wallcases are made as four-sided pine boxes stained walnut and finished with a natural brown fir plywood or Masonite back. By using thicker 2 inch × 8 inch wood shelves, 4-foot widths could be used without the annoying problem of sagging. The result was larger individual fixture bays and one-third less number of fixtures to be installed.

In the second phase, an academic and scholarly book department with a raised gallery (6), a classical record department (7), and a discounted paperback bestsellers department (8) were added to the first floor. The paperback department was enlarged and sections were set up to display a stock of thousands of new classical records, tapes, and educational and scholarly reference books from accounting to zoology. Book Ends, a closeout department, was located in space found in the basement (9).

7

8

9

1

2

3

4

5

6

BARNES & NOBLE SALES ANNEX

UPTOWN—RADIO CITY
NEW YORK, NY

THE UPTOWN STORE, as it is known, was built on Fifth Avenue at 48th Street in Radio City. It moved away from the dark look of the first Sales Annex to an altogether different light and airy interior look. The 22,000-square-foot space, formerly occupied by a quality men's clothier, was converted into a comfortable browsing and bookselling place in record time and cost.

As part of the $750,000 renovation cost, the existing bronze and granite store front was enlarged to include a second statuary bronze revolving door (1). On the street level, an existing travertine marble-surfaced circulation aisle was retained and bound by a carpeted floor which reaches to the perimeter walls (2). There, sets of *The Encyclopedia Britannica,* adult games, discount paperbacks (3), children's, how-to, and New York city guides and related books surround the parcel check, control turnstiles, escalators, central promotional space, and a bank of eight checkout stations. The checkout area can, on demand, be expanded to accommodate 10 cashier stations.

The New York Times bestsellers (4), animals and nature (5), and Abrams art books (6), are located on the main (basement) floor with the service desk and general and scholarly hardbound remainder book departments.

The three-level selling plan placed the discount classical record and tape department on an open mezzanine overlooking the street floor (7).

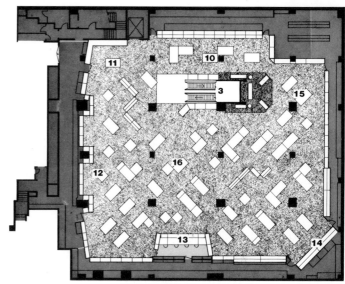

MAIN FLOOR (Lower Level)

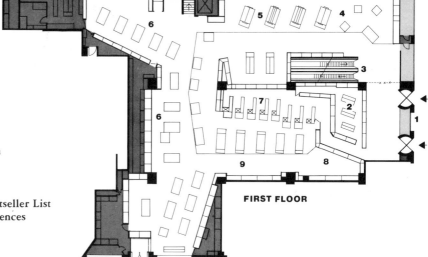

FIRST FLOOR

1

NEW CANAAN
BOOKSHOP

NEW CANAAN, CT

THE NEW CANAAN BOOKSHOP presents one of the best book collections in the Northeast. But if you can imagine moving a bookstore to another temporary location across the street while the building you had occupied was demolished and a new one constructed, then you can imagine the complications of this project.

Once we had designed and coordinated the building concept, its exterior materials, and graphics (1), a modified diagonal plan was developed to facilitate customer flow from the front, deep into the store to a lovely children's book section (2) in this pleasant 4,000-square-foot shop. The plan for this warm wood and weathered-brick bookshop also provides for stationery, cards for all occasions, party supplies, desk accessories, and gift items.

The sales space is visually divided into three sales rooms by oak-trimmed beams (3). The lighting is restrained. Low surface brightness fluorescent fixtures trimmed with oak frames are surface-mounted throughout the sales area. The high oak-stained book wallcases, in keeping with the design criteria of this easy-to-maintain, full-service bookshop, are open and lighted at the top.

3

2

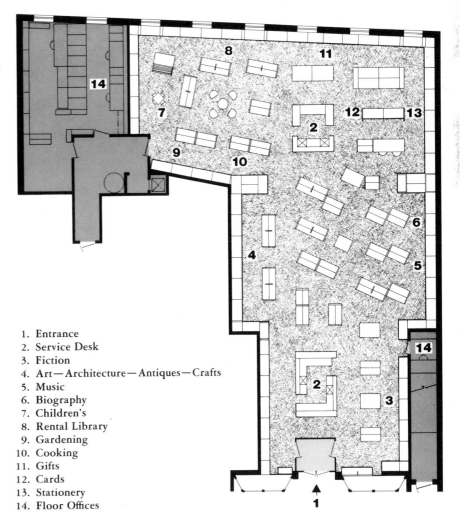

1. Entrance
2. Service Desk
3. Fiction
4. Art—Architecture—Antiques—Crafts
5. Music
6. Biography
7. Children's
8. Rental Library
9. Gardening
10. Cooking
11. Gifts
12. Cards
13. Stationery
14. Floor Offices

120   PART 2

UCONN CO-OP

UNIVERSITY OF CONNECTICUT
STORRS, CT

IT SEEMED TO EVERYONE INVOLVED that the new UConn Co-op building was a long time coming. But the reality is that Ray Verrey and the Co-op staff of the youngest of the cooperative university bookstores were able to develop a successful business and build their new building in 5 short years (1).

Situated where it comfortably coexists with a neighboring brown brick university library, the bookstore space is divided into two levels— 20,000 square feet of retailing on the first floor and 5,000 square feet of processing (2), receiving, and skylighted office space (3) on the lower level.

The building is a pleasing design of purpose, strength, and taste. It is a windowless steel-framed structure faced with a skin of Alucabond, large monolithic panels of an especially bonded and treated aluminum material. The entrance to the building is covered by an expansive Alucabond-faced shed thrusting out from the building to provide weather protection for the long ramp and tiled stairs leading up to the sales level.

Entering the new store, the customer is welcomed by a white graphic on a bronze Plexiglas background (4) which also announces that all books and parcels are to be checked in book drops, coin return lockers, or at the service desk straight ahead. A large, multicolored graphic map over the service desk of the store makes it simple for first-time shoppers to locate major departments.

A modified angular planning arrangement with a loop traffic aisle pattern encircles the entire interior of the store, leading past the perimeter and central core departments. This version of the yellow brick road provides a natural division of the selling space into general (5) and course books, stationery, soft goods, imprint and insignia ware, greeting card, supply, and graphic art departments. The aisle also leads to "Goodies," a partially enclosed shop where food, beverages, candy, and refrigerated snacks are featured.

The best architectural experience of this building comes, however, when the customer walks from the entrance into the book departments. There, three very wide clerestories of translucent plastic admit natural light into the sales space (6).

The white walls of the general book department reach up 10 feet high above a raised gallery and are united by a continuous cinnamon-colored

4

5

6

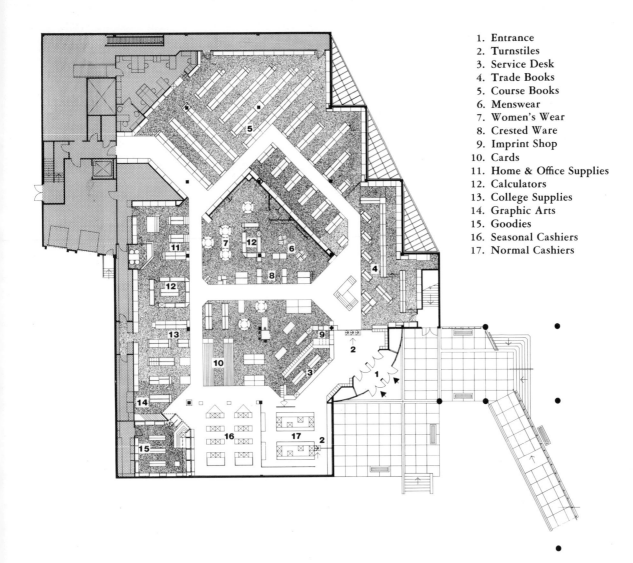

1. **Entrance**
2. **Turnstiles**
3. **Service Desk**
4. **Trade Books**
5. **Course Books**
6. **Menswear**
7. **Women's Wear**
8. **Crested Ware**
9. **Imprint Shop**
10. **Cards**
11. **Home & Office Supplies**
12. **Calculators**
13. **College Supplies**
14. **Graphic Arts**
15. **Goodies**
16. **Seasonal Cashiers**
17. **Normal Cashiers**

7

8

cornice and graphic band, but float free of the 14-foot-high exposed structural ceiling. A soft gray color on the walls above the fixturing is repeated in the carpet in this department.

The course book department is surrounded by high red oak wallcases on a mahogany-colored carpet. The deep color of the floor covering delineates the almond-colored floor gondola fixtures. The department is color-coded—each major book section is identified with a graphic flag suspended from the ceiling with thin aircraft cable.

The stationery, supply, and graphic art department has its own special ambiance. It is beige and gold, with dark bronze graphic backgrounds and painted showcases. Soft goods—the women's (7) and menswear (8) department—incorporates the latest visual merchandising techniques using faceout merchandisers on oak panel walls, tables, and circular two-way and four-way adjustable racks.

Chrome-plated towers set on stepped burgundy-colored lacquer platforms support glass shelves for the display of crested gift and glassware.

The color palette of Goodies (9) is simple but effective. Rough-sawn natural fir wallcases trimmed with cinnamon and white are complemented by a spiced-briar-colored carpet.

The aisle ends at the hub of the store's normal cashiering activity: two permanent checkout islands with a total of eight electronic data collecting cash registers (10). But twice a year for the school opening rush periods, the Co-op gears up to serve the 22,000 University of Connecticut students with their books and supplies (11), the bulk of which are sold during a frenzied 3-day period. Then, 16 additional registers are moved in on eight table-type cash stands arranged in a piggyback fashion. Once this hectic period is over, these temporary cash registers are removed and the space is converted to retailing use. With this flexibility, the merchandise managers can make quick marketing and service changes without appearing to be pressing too hard—rather like the building itself.

9

10

11

1

2

BARNES & NOBLE

WESTFARMS SHOPPING MALL
CORBINS CORNER, CT

FOR ITS FIRST BOOKSTORE to be located in a major regional shopping mall, Barnes & Noble leased 3,800 square feet of usable space and commissioned our firm to plan and design a unique, fully integrated shop consistent with their merchandising concept and the quality standards of the Westfarms Mall.

The natural wood and earth tones of this successful bookstore begin at the front of the store. The proscenium of the front is faced with squares of Gothic oak parquet flooring, laminated to the structural surfaces (1) of the angular-fronted store, which fits in comfortably with its neighbors in the mall. One hue of carpet begins at the front and covers the main floor surface to the rear. It is divided by three wide bands of a second contrasting color carpet into four sections. The second color covers the steps, selling area, and open manager's office on the gallery.

The chief virtue of the design of this typical long, narrow space is the angular planning arrangement with high staggered bookcases (2) on the right wall and a gallery raised 2 feet above the sales floor on the left. The idea of these elements is to create interesting sight lines to break up the long tunnel-like view into the store. The angular arrangement leads browsers deep into the store. The absence of rows upon rows of gondolas arranged in the traditional grid layout is significant. The different approach was to use higher gondolas with more shelf capacity to form a third selling wall along the edge of the raised gallery. This makes room for the angled, rimmed-top sale tables and cubes (4). Twenty percent of the mall store floor space is devoted to a unique mix of children's books and educational materials.

1. Entrance
2. Service/Cashier Desk
3. Office
4. Gallery
5. Bestsellers
6. Cooking
7. Children's
8. Receiving & Storage

3

4

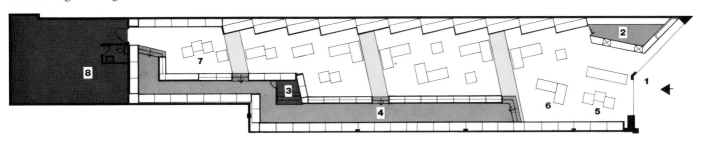

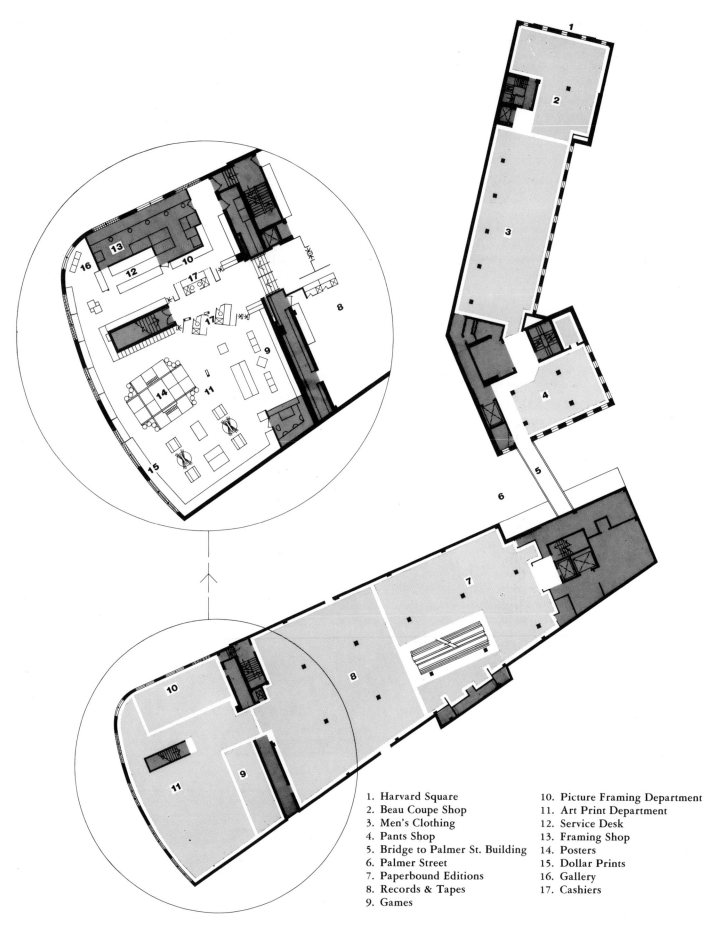

1. Harvard Square
2. Beau Coupe Shop
3. Men's Clothing
4. Pants Shop
5. Bridge to Palmer St. Building
6. Palmer Street
7. Paperbound Editions
8. Records & Tapes
9. Games
10. Picture Framing Department
11. Art Print Department
12. Service Desk
13. Framing Shop
14. Posters
15. Dollar Prints
16. Gallery
17. Cashiers

THE HARVARD COOP

HARVARD SQUARE
CAMBRIDGE, MA

Constant change has become a condition of business at the Harvard Coop. Until the middle 1970s, the Coop had long been famed as America's largest bookstore. The 124,120-square-foot store contains 24 complete deparments with a range of goods featuring trade, text, reference books, and national-brand merchandise. Anyone may shop at the Coop, which honors all major credit cards (but prefers customers to use its own) and provides parking at Harvard Square, MIT, and the Medical Center.

The Coop owns and operates its main store at Harvard Square. The main store is, in fact, part of a larger complex that includes the MIT Coop, the Law, Medical, and Graduate School of Business Coop stores—five in all. We designed these stores and the late Coop general manager, John Morrill, built all of them within a 7-year period. But every year changes and additions are made by new general managers to keep pace with a fast-changing and competitive market.

Book and art print sales are conducted in a five-story building directly across Palmer Street at the rear of the main store. The book building is connected to the main building by a tunnel and pedestrian bridge under and over Palmer Street.

All books are arranged in basic subject categories for customer convenience on the first floor, where children's (1), fiction (2), and general hardbound trade books (3) are marketed on ledge-type library-like wallcases, tables, and gondolas of English oak.

The Coop has an outstanding record department (4) with an extraordinary assortment of classical, pop, language, and specialty records and tapes, an attraction which has drawn several thousand people onto the second floor of the store on a single Saturday. The same floor contains paperback editions (5), educational games, and the Coop Art Print Department (6, 7).

Crossing over the bridge to the main store, customers move through to the men's pants shop, a clothing department featuring (what else) Ivy League suits, jackets, and coats (8), and the Beau Coop Shop, a specialty merchandising section (9).

Reference, science, technical, and general course books are sold on the third floor of the Palmer Street Building (10).

1

2

3

4

5

6

Coop departments include:

- Accessories
- Art prints
- Cameras and film
- Cosmetics
- Creative toys
- Domestics
- General hardbound trade books
- Household remedies
- Housewares
- Lingerie
- Luggage
- Men's boutique
- Men's clothing
- Men's furnishings
- Men's shoes
- Misses' sportswear
- Office supplies
- Paperback books
- Records
- Science, technology, and course books
- Stationery
- TVs and radios
- Typewriters

Coop services include:

- Alterations
- Coop charge card
- Gift wrapping
- Optical department
- Picture framing
- Typewriter and equipment rentals

7

8

9

10

1

2

3

4

5

6

THE TECH COOP OF THE HARVARD COOPERATIVE SOCIETY IN THE MIT STUDENT CENTER

CAMBRIDGE, MA

CAMBRIDGE IS the classical college town, a suburb of Boston and home of the Massachusetts Institute of Technology. Here, the Tech Coop occupies 30,000 square feet in the MIT Student Center—25,000 square feet on the main floor and 5,000 square feet on the lower level. This Harvard Coop branch is a miniature version of the main Harvard Square store.

The building is made of raw concrete with an exposed "waffle" ceiling, which is relieved by an acoustically treated dropped ceiling over the record, stationery, and supply departments (1). The U-shaped selling space creates a natural division of the book (2) and nonbook departments.

The interior of the Tech Coop is a study in monotones intended to provide a neutral visual merchandising background. There are only two colors used in the space: the matte white walls and textured gray carpet. The wood is white oak and the departmental signs are gold-lettered on putty gray backgrounds.

1. Entrance
2. Service Desks
3. Check Cashing & Cashier
4. Check-out Stations
5. Controlled Sales Islands
6. Stationery & Supplies
7. Health & Beauty Aids
8. Home Furnishings
9. Men's Clothing & Furnishings
10. Records & Tapes
11. Paperbound Editions
12. Course & Reference Books
13. Lobby Shop

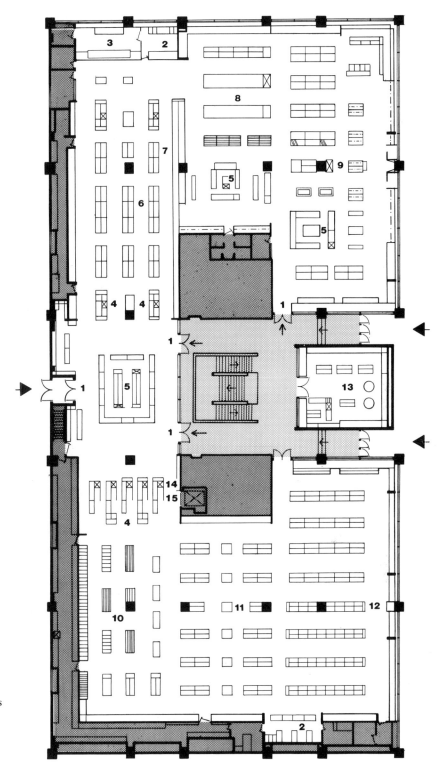

1

2

THE CONTRACT DESIGN CENTER BOOKSHOP

CHICAGO, IL

THE CONTRACT DESIGN CENTER BOOKSHOP and Gallery, a specialty shop which opened on the eleventh floor of Chicago's prestigious Merchandise Mart in 1,300 square feet of space, is the home of some of the latest and most interesting design ideas in small bookshop (4), reference library (6), and gallery (3) architecture that we have produced. Unlike most other bookstores and libraries, the Contract Design Center is designed to serve designers, architects, and specifiers of contract furnishings.

Manfred Steinfeld, chairman of Shelby Williams Industries, knew when he saw the jostling crowd in the bookstalls of London's Design Centre that a similar facility would be a useful resource for the design community in the United States. He found a place for it by leasing space adjacent to his showroom in Chicago's Merchandise Mart. The bookshop is entered from the showroom, past a display of design books in stepped glass cubes, into the sales area (1). The bookshop is contained in a simple arrangement occupying 800 square feet of the space. The main circulation flows up a ramped gallery, past curved sales tables, low brass etageres, and high-low gondolas (7), to a semicircular library and on to a product gallery stocked with samples (2) and (5).

When developing the idea, I saw a close parallel between a product gallery and an art gallery of the type popularized by the Rizzoli International Bookstores. They are, after all, both literary oases. The Rizzoli Bookstores are cosmopolitan; the Contract Design Center is technical. The Rizzoli Gallery events focus on art, sculpture, and photographic shows. The Contract Design Center and Product Gallery follows a similar concept, but its emphasis is on applied arts, design, and technical reference books. Its gallery shows are industrial and graphic in nature.

The color scheme in the bookshop is monochromatic with creamy white floor tiles, custom sand-colored cut pile carpet, and red oak, with mirror, brass, and scarlet accents.

3

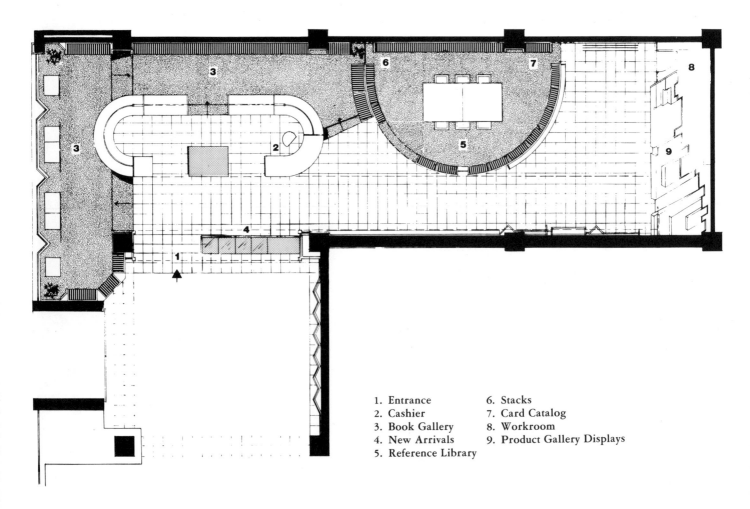

1. Entrance
2. Cashier
3. Book Gallery
4. New Arrivals
5. Reference Library
6. Stacks
7. Card Catalog
8. Workroom
9. Product Gallery Displays

6

7

RIZZOLI INTERNATIONAL BOOKSTORE OF CHICAGO

CHICAGO, IL.

2

Located on the third level of Watertower Plaza, on the glamorous near north side of Michigan Boulevard in Chicago, this store was the first U.S. Rizzoli International Bookstore and Gallery to be built outside of New York City. Because the Rizzoli stores are thought of as culture centers rather than bookstores, many of the visual elements of the classical New York store were carried forward to Chicago, including the travertine marble show window facings (2), foyer floors, and entrance details. The emerald green cut pile carpet and bronze metal finishes followed. Brass cornice plaques and stone artifacts from Italy arrived shortly thereafter.

But the Chicago Rizzoli store has many of its own features, one of which is the cold cathode indirect lighting system concealed in overhead beams, which illuminates the main sales area of the bookstore (3). However, it is the elegant and traditional sculptured marble entrance door with its detail and frame that is the architectural feature of this store (1). The principal design concept for the store was furnished to us by Rizzoli; it originated in Italy and arrived in the form of large drawings made in meters at a scale of approximately 1/2 inch to the foot. For our staff, it was the beginning of an interesting project: to reduce and translate the drawings made overseas, coordinating them with ideas and merchandising information developed by Gianfranco Monacelli, the North American general manager of the Rizzoli Editore Corporation. Our end product was a set of workable drawings and details for the fixture construction of this 5,700-square-foot bookstore.

The Rizzoli International Bookstore and Gallery of Chicago opened with a marvelous champagne party. It offers its customers a fine selection of books on art, dance, music, theater, and fashion; and beautiful gift books and specialty items. The pleasant surroundings, wide aisles, late Baroque background music, marvelous collections of books, and the services of an attentive, multilingual staff provide an appropriate atmosphere for bibliophiles.

3

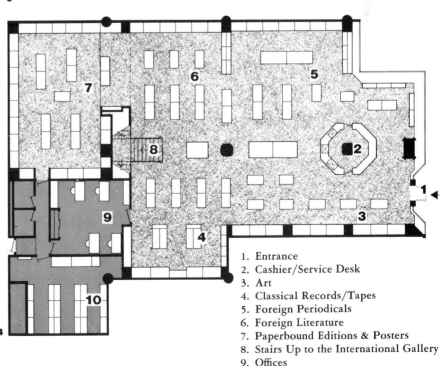

1. Entrance
2. Cashier/Service Desk
3. Art
4. Classical Records/Tapes
5. Foreign Periodicals
6. Foreign Literature
7. Paperbound Editions & Posters
8. Stairs Up to the International Gallery
9. Offices
10. Receiving/Shipping/Processing

YOUR BOOKSTORE THE INDIANA MEMORIAL UNION

INDIANA UNIVERSITY
BLOOMINGTON, IN

I T IS A RARE DAY that you will not find a steady stream of students, faculty, alumni, and visitors browsing and shopping in this 31,000-square-foot bookstore. Your Bookstore is housed in a beautiful Gothic building (1), which in many respects fulfills the notion of a college store that is visually the ideal academic bookstore.

The space is divided into three sales floors. On the lower level, an impressive display of text, trade, and reference books is featured, stocked, and serviced by an informed and attentive staff. The main floor contains soft goods, art, stationery, cards, gifts, and jewelry departments. The mezzanine level rings the first floor with record (2), electronics, print and frame, magazine, sale book, and plant (3) departments that have something for every imaginable taste in their broad selection. But the real point of Your Bookstore is that it is well organized in a space that is a joy to browse in.

The planning and design task was laid out by Bill Turk, the manager, who said, "This building was designed with real style. The architects used high-quality workmanship and first-rate materials. We are very concerned not to disturb that balance."

1

2

The soaring Gothic cathedral ceilings, arched limestone openings, and heavy oak railings encircling the balcony are softened by the red traditional design carpet and soft beige wall surfaces. The plant department (3), all stained glass windows, and academic flags hung in the atrium add color accents to the subtle color scheme.

3

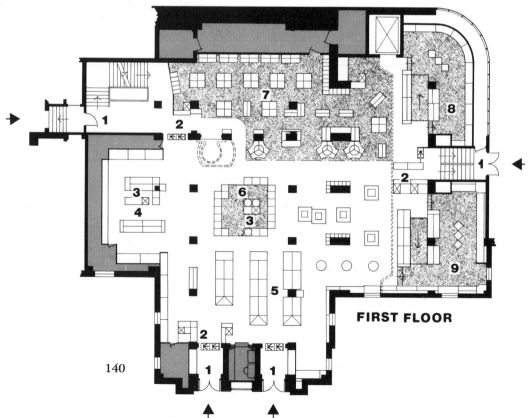

FIRST FLOOR

140

FIRST FLOOR

1. Entrance
2. Check-out
3. Controlled Sales
4. Art
5. Cards
6. Jewelry
7. Softgoods
8. Stationery
9. Supplies

MEZZANINE PLAN

10. Electronics
11. Records
12. Live Plants
13. Art Prints
14. Magazines
15. Sale Books
16. Check Cashing

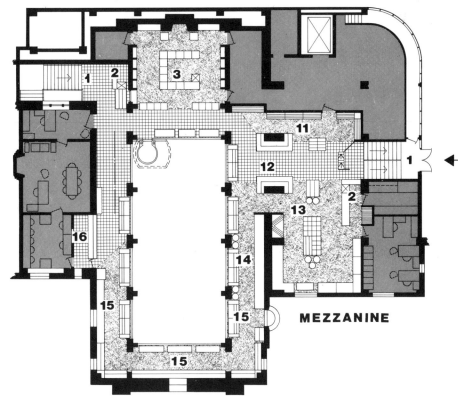

MEZZANINE

1

THE MINNESOTA BOOK CENTER

MINNEAPOLIS, MN

In 1978, the Minnesota Book Center opened for student shoppers on the − 2 floor level of a new underground, solar-heated building—Williamson Hall—located on the main campus of the University of Minnesota. The 84,000-square-foot collage of public space, offices, and bookstore was heralded as an innovative departure from routine bookstore and student service office building design. In operation, the store has lived up to every expectation of Jim Duffy, manager, planner, and prime mover of the project. The University of Minnesota Bookstore is ranked the sixth largest volume college store operation in the United States.

The $4.3 million building is square, bisected at ground level by a concrete walkway. One floor below grade (− 1 level), an interior concourse provides a panoramic view down into the bookstore (1), bright with sunlight from clerestory windows, and an interior courtyard. Bookstore customers travel down banks of escalators and pass through sliding glass doors (2) to reach the sales level of the three-story-high, 21,000-square-foot bookselling emporium. Duffy and his management team oversee a four-store complex of university-owned bookstore facilities. The executive offices (3) and staff lounge are located on a balcony (− 1 level) which overlooks the sunlit atrium bookstore, resembling an indoor park complete with its 25-foot-high trees.

Inside walls and ceiling—like the outside—are rough concrete. But in the bookstore 20 percent of the floor is raised and ramped to two gallery bookselling levels (4), each covered with a different hue of brown carpet and wood store fixturing, a counterpoint to the concrete texture. Bold primary-colored graphic panels and neatly detailed custom-built wood (5) and utilitarian metal store fixtures (6, 7), colored in earth tones, are elegant in this setting.

2

4

3

5

6

7

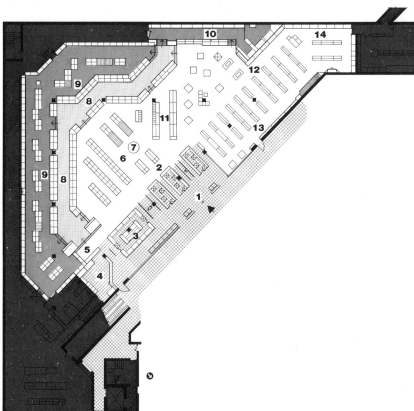

1. Entrance
2. Check-outs
3. Controlled Sales
4. Service Desk
5. Scholarship Charges
6. Course Books
7. Trees
8. First Gallery
9. Second Gallery
10. Softgoods Gallery
11. Supply Department
12. Gifts
13. Trade Books
14. Cards

1

2

3

4

6

BOOKS UNDERGROUND

UNIVERSITY OF MINNESOTA
ST. PAUL, MN

7

U PON ENTERING this second new underground bookstore, the impact of the interior is apparent. The store, which opened in the fall of 1979, is located in an underground building of exposed concrete, glass, and brick, and is appropriately named Books Underground. The store is oriented to one side of a sloping, brick-paved underground street or corridor, which has one wall of glass and glass displays facing the 6,700-square-foot bookstore (1). From this heavily trafficked underground street there are generous views into the bookstore, with its life and activity in the retail sales space.

The space is molded and contoured with a series of large consecutive platforms connected with easy access ramps and steps for handicapped persons, that lead into trade, reference, and course book merchandising galleries (2). Natural light is filtered through light shafts with translucent plastic ceilings and an expansive glass entrance to the building, visible from the store. An exposed concrete ceiling is relieved with panels of light wood slats that frame the ceiling of the space at both ends of the store (3).

The background is an earth tone color scheme of chocolate brown brick pavers, chestnut carpet, and red oak counters and book fixtures (4, 5). Vibrantly colored metal supply department fixtures and cubes add accent color to this monochromatic color scheme. Polished chrome merchandisers (6) and glass towers set on cube bases (7) are used in place of traditional gondolas.

1. Entrance
2. Trade Book Gallery
3. Service Desk
4. Reference Books
5. Ramps
6. Course Book Gallery
7. Softgoods
8. Gifts
9. Cards
10. Supplies
11. Crafts
12. Office
13. Cashiers

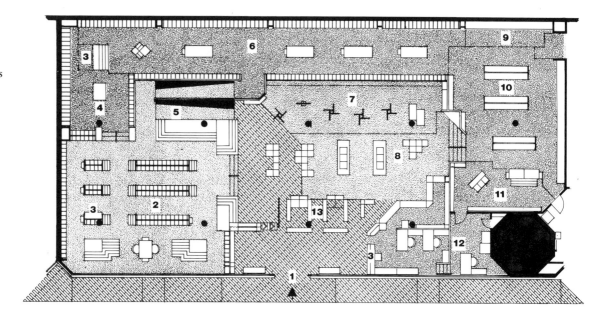

GPO U.S. GOVERNMENT BOOKSTORE

ARCO PLAZA
LOS ANGELES, CA

THIS GOVERNMENT PRINTING OFFICE bookstore is a highly specialized shop with the facility to show face out 2,000 of the 22,000 titles published by the organization. Mounds and stacks of book pamphlets and periodicals are the feature of the design in this pleasing new 3,000-square-foot space located on Level C of the Arco Plaza in downtown Los Angeles.

The mission of the Government Printing Office bookstores is to make government documents available to the general public, and to stock the categories of books and materials that will appeal to the residents of a given region in the country. That accounts for the large number of solar energy, home gardening, and building technology books on the store's new shelves, as well as the beautifully illustrated space exploration books and maps that are of high interest in the Los Angeles region.

The shop was designed to be "people pleasing" but not faddish; to have a simple, clean cut look about it. One of the unique display features is a pair of etageres placed on tables next to graduated step display units at the front of the store (1).

Once inside the space, the sales room develops into an L-shaped area lined with book stacks from floor to ceiling. The high stacks serviced from rolling ladders, to take advantage of the "air space" in the store, contain greater stock capacity and thus reduce the amount of valuable selling area needed for reserve stock purposes. A book beam is employed to visually divide the floor into three selling areas which present collections of federal regulations and reference materials. The arrangement of store fixturing is placed to lead the customer in an orderly sequence through the selling area to the service area. Here, the elements of cashiering, customer service, and manager's office space are consolidated to minimize the space occupied by these functional activities.

At the front of the space the floor is surfaced with burnt orange color quarry tile. A stone grey carpet unifies the major sales space. The perimeter walls, book beams, and floor selling equipment were carefully detailed and made of a warm tone of red oak. A color pallet of twine and grey with cinnamon accents was used for wall panels, cornices, and graphic backgrounds. The continuous service counter top is a neutral sand-colored, durable work surface.

2

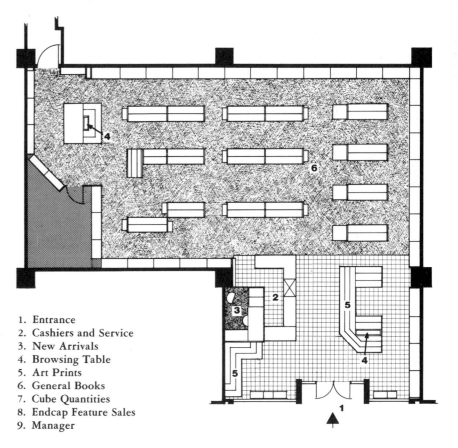

1. Entrance
2. Cashiers and Service
3. New Arrivals
4. Browsing Table
5. Art Prints
6. General Books
7. Cube Quantities
8. Endcap Feature Sales
9. Manager

1

2

UNIVERSITY BOOKSTORE

THE UNIVERSITY OF NEW MEXICO
ALBUQUERQUE, NM

THE UNIVERSITY OF NEW MEXICO Bookstore presents an entirely different notion of what the image and form of its academic bookstore building should be and the nature of the 26,000-square-foot bookstore it contains.

The design concept of this store was to maintain a low profile and not compete with the other large structures in the immediate vicinity. The main book sales area is – 1 level below grade. The administration area and nonbook sales departments are located at grade level (1). This arrangement allows visual control from the mezzanine (2) by the administrative personnel. Sunlight filters into the lower selling level through nine bronze-tinted, pyramid-shaped skylights banked together in the main ceiling over the integrated book departments. Other pyramid skylights allow natural light to effectively beam past the gift department ceiling (3) and drop through an open triangular well to the lower level supply department. The roof of the bookstore forms a plaza connecting directly to a concourse which links a lecture hall, the Humanities Building, and the Student Union with the Art Building (4). The entrance to the bookstore from the roof plaza serves also as a means for exiting from the concourse to ground level by elevator for handicapped persons.

3

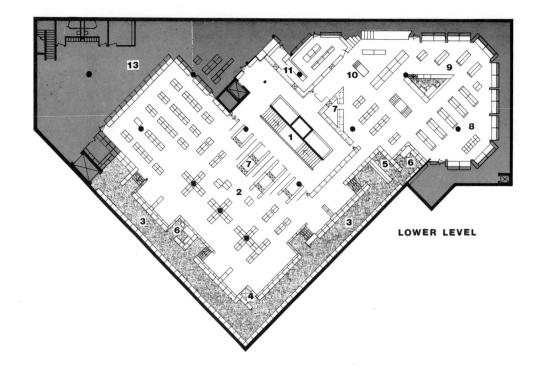

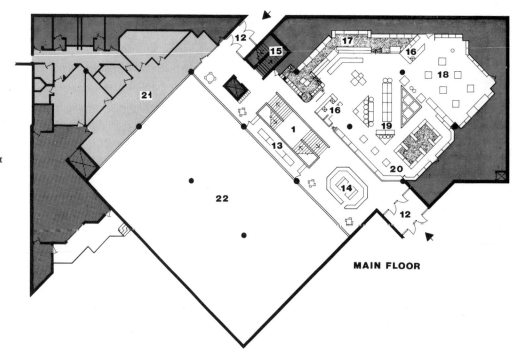

All the books, including class texts, reference and trade, and new and used titles, are integrated, arranged by subject matter, and identified with simple graphics in this emporium managed by A. O. Jackson. This merchandising concept made it possible to bring together and correlate all the reading materials at the high-ceilinged end of the

4

5

store and to locate the remaining art, supply, campus wear, and gift departments on the two selling levels at the opposite end. There is a comfortable air about the University of New Mexico Bookstore. It is, in fact, a very special place.

1

2

GPO U.S. GOVERNMENT BOOKSTORE

HOUSTON, TX

UNLIKE MOST OTHER BOOKSTORES, there is a bookshop in Texas that doesn't have a single bestseller on its shelves. Instead, you can find a sample of the books offered by one of the nation's oldest and biggest publishers, the U.S. government. The store is located in a suburban shopping center and was the first GPO bookstore in the United States outside federal office buildings (1). The reason is to make the GPO's inventory of 25,000 titles more accessible to the public.

Built on three gallery levels, the oak store fixtures were designed to accommodate the thousands of brochures and softbound books published by the GPO. The space is visually organized with a warm color scheme and category graphic system.

Categories offered by the government range from "Accidents and Aviation" (2), to "Rockets and Space" (3). There are also hundreds of how-to books and brochures on subjects that range from farming to weather forecasting. The GPO bookstores sell a lot of textbooks to colleges and universities, but the overall best seller is the national zip code directory.

3

1. Entrance
2. Cashiers
3. Floor Office
4. Ramps
5. First Gallery
6. Manager's Open Office
7. Second Gallery
8. Prints
9. Cube Displays
10. Hi-Lo Gondolas
11. Processing
12. Receiving/Shipping

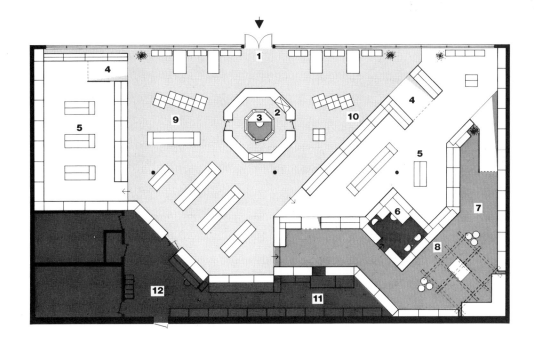

1

2

3

J. NORTH BOOKSELLER

FORT WORTH, TX

AMEDIUM-SIZED, 2,000-square-foot store with wall-to-wall and floor-to-ceiling displays of books, this stylish bookstore specializes in quality hardcover and trade paperback books. With the opening of the shop came the fulfillment of Janis North's life ambition to own her own bookstore, and that accounts for the special ambiance and personal touch found here.

Diagonal-pattern flooring leads from the front door, past stacks and mounds of new arrivals and bestsellers, to the service desk (1). The English style of the store results from a few special details such as the service desk, made of wood with a leatherlike pattern top. The face of the desk is trimmed and embellished with carved wood rope and pattern moldings. Other details include a large wood browsing table and antique country English chairs (2).

But the major unifying design elements in this bookshop are the high, mellow mahogany wallcases surrounding the walls. The main literature sections are stocked on a raised and carpeted gallery, furnished with traditional occasional chairs (3).

Children's books are important in this store. Located in one corner facing the entrance door, this department occupies 20 percent of the total store's selling space (4). The large section is divided by age group up to teens. The focal point of the department is a children's book cave. The lighted and carpeted cave takes up a tiny amount of space, but it is one of the nice touches that make this successful shop a pleasant place in which to spend time and browse.

1. **Entrance**
2. **Cashier/Service Desk**
3. **Lending Library**
4. **Browsing Table**
5. **Gallery**
6. **Children's Cave**
7. **Hi-Lo Gondolas**
8. **Receiving/Shipping/Processing**

4

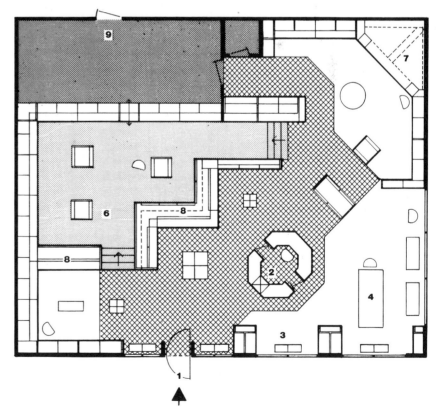

1

RIZZOLI INTERNATIONAL BOOKSTORE OF ATLANTA, GA

LOCATED ON THE SECOND LEVEL of Atlanta's Omni International Center, this Rizzoli Bookstore is marked by restrained elegance and its formal style. Although the store is large, 7,200 square feet, it is made to seem even larger by the use of a well-proportioned glass front extending the full width of the space (1). The bold design of the front emphasizes strong horizontal lines with travertine marble, bronze, and glass; yet the store is a comfortable place. Store services and controls are administered from a hexagonal control counter of dark oak (2) at the front of the store.

The quality classical record and tape department (3), which features folk music from around the

2

3

1. Entrance
2. Cashiers/Service Desk
3. Art
4. Reference
5. Classical Records/Tapes
6. Paperbound Editions/Prints
7. Stairs Up to the International Gallery
8. Foreign Periodicals
9. Literature
10. Administrative Offices
11. Receiving/Shipping/Processing

world, not customarily available in Atlanta, visually echos the paperback department (4) with its dark oak, bronze, and emerald green carpet color scheme.

A double entry stair links the two-level space, rising one level from the main floor (5) to the international art gallery (6). Rizzoli regularly exhibits photographs by local artists, sponsors autograph parties, and hosts readings by local poets.

Although their primary interest is in art books—the Italian parent company is an art publisher—they also stock domestic fiction and nonfiction titles. But foreign titles are the store's specialty. The main foreign language collections are French, German, Spanish, and Italian.

Students, professors, visitors to Omni International, and transplanted New Yorkers who enjoy browsing and shopping in the store are Rizzoli's typical customers.

4

5

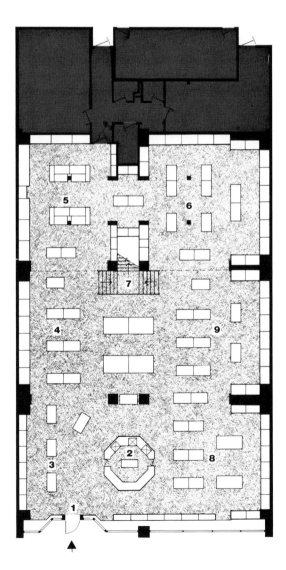

6

1

2

160 PART 2

GEORGIA TECH BOOKSTORE

GEORGIA INSTITUTE OF TECHNOLOGY
ATLANTA, GA

THE GEORGIA TECH BOOKSTORE is situated on one 20,000-square-foot selling level and is nearly surrounded with generously sized perimeter stockrooms. Architecturally, the building is a gem. The monolithic red brick exterior is relieved with well-proportioned pilasters and a chamfered parapet which give form and class to this compact building (1). The red brick, repeated in the walls and walks, flows into the entrance lobby. There, brick is used to sheath the columns and exposed walls of the busy entrance and cashier areas (2).

The interior circulation revolves within the grid plan around a sunken pit located between the four main supporting columns and a skylight in the book department in this hospitable academic bookstore. The atmosphere is a meld of filtered natural light, neutral color, plants, and bold graphic accents.

The Tech Bookstore features one of the largest collections of fiction and nonfiction books found in college stores of its size, with easy-to-find sections of quality paperbacks and hardcovers.

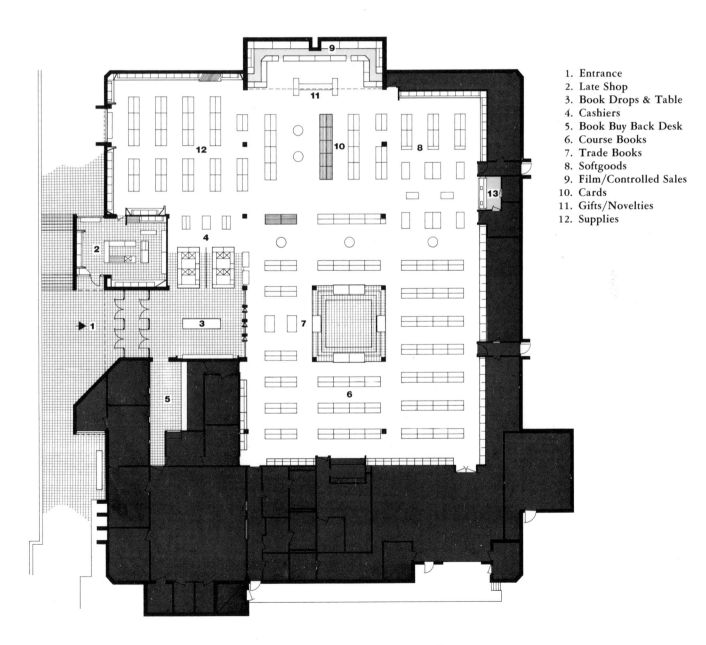

1. Entrance
2. Late Shop
3. Book Drops & Table
4. Cashiers
5. Book Buy Back Desk
6. Course Books
7. Trade Books
8. Softgoods
9. Film/Controlled Sales
10. Cards
11. Gifts/Novelties
12. Supplies

1

2

3

UNIVERSITY BOOKSTORE

VIRGINIA TECH
BLACKSBURG, VA

THE VIRGINIA TECH UNIVERSITY BOOKSTORE is a four-level, glassed-in space. It is an extraordinarily handsome 25,000-square-foot bookstore. The new building is stylish (1). The three selling levels and mezzanine office floors were shaped into a steel and stone structure, and carefully tucked into a site controlled by large rock formations. But the essence of the building is the academic bookstore it contains.

The bookstore building is entered through a high lobby with stone and glass walls opening to a view of the first floor book galleries and mezzanine office level of the building. Inside, the random-pattern stone floor is joined by carpet for its acoustical value, color, and texture contrast.

When the customer walks from the first floor lobby to the lower level, past the book drops and cashiers, the upper lobby becomes, in effect, a promenade. The stairs with their massive oak railings appear to turn first to the left and then to the right without giving the impression of a store burdened with an endless number of steps (2). A passenger elevator is provided for handicapped customers.

Books are located in three tiered galleries, raised up and connected to the main floor by gentle ramps and steps provided with nicely detailed chrome tubing railings (3). As a convenience for students shopping on this level, school and stationery supplies are adjacent to the book departments. Cards, records, sundries, film, and jewelry are housed on the intermediate level midway between the first and lower floors (4). The space has been shaped to create an unusual architectural experience and to enhance the retailing ambiance.

There is a second entrance to the building on the lower level. There, art is situated in its own gallery (5), and sporting goods, gifts and novelties, and softwear (6) are displayed in a series of shop and boutique arrangements. The columns contained on the lower level are mirrored for esthetic and security purposes.

4

5

6

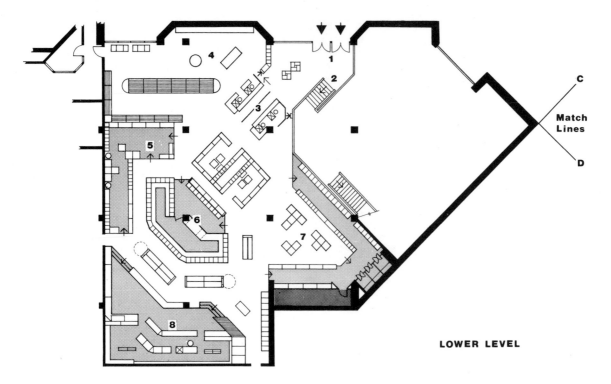

LOWER LEVEL

LOWER LEVEL
1. Entrance
2. Stairs Up
3. Check-outs
4. Cards
5. Gifts/Novelties
6. Imprint Shop
7. Campus Wear
8. Art

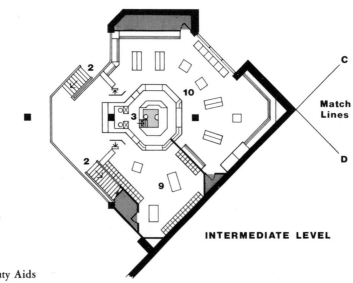

INTERMEDIATE LEVEL

INTERMEDIATE LEVEL
9. Record Shop
10. Snacks/Health & Beauty Aids

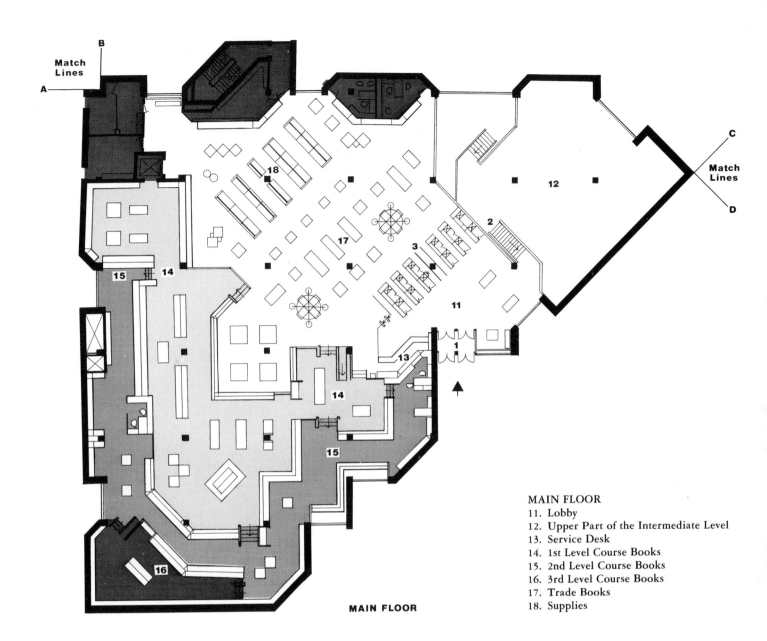

MAIN FLOOR
11. Lobby
12. Upper Part of the Intermediate Level
13. Service Desk
14. 1st Level Course Books
15. 2nd Level Course Books
16. 3rd Level Course Books
17. Trade Books
18. Supplies

MAIN FLOOR

MEZZANINE

MEZZANINE LEVEL
19. Employee Lounge
20. General Office
21. Conference Room
22. Office
23. Accounting
24. Director's Office

1

DUKE MEDICAL BOOKSTORE

RALEIGH, NC

LOCATED INSIDE the G. Mudd Medical Library building on the Duke University Campus, this store specializes in and carries a large selection of books covering all aspects of medicine, nursing, and allied health professions. In addition to a large selection of textbooks for students, the store stocks a fine list of carefully selected medical and biomedical reference books for graduate students and practitioners of medicine, dentistry, and nursing. The 2,000-square-foot angular store is a major educational resource, serving both the local area and the Middle Atlantic states.

The floor is surfaced with a diagonal-patterned white oak parquet, accented by an Oriental rug in the browsing area (1). There are two ceiling heights in the store. The low, 9-foot-high ceiling over the front entrance of the store is planked with cedar boards. The 16-foot-high, smooth concrete ceiling that is exposed in the rest of the store is painted white. The perimeter walls are faced with high ledge bookcases served by rolling ladders (2). These ladders are used by the bookstore staff for access to reserve books concealed in storage cabinets behind hinged oak doors above the neatly detailed bookcases in the high-ceilinged area.

The hexagonal oak control desk has a raised, carpeted floor and contains two work stations, lighted glass showcases, and built-in cashier stations (3). The continuous oak counter is finished at the top with a contrasting black granite ledge.

The ambience of the space is reinforced by reflected daylight through large high windows (4), plants, leather browsing chairs, oak flooring, Oriental rugs, and shelves and stacks of beautiful books.

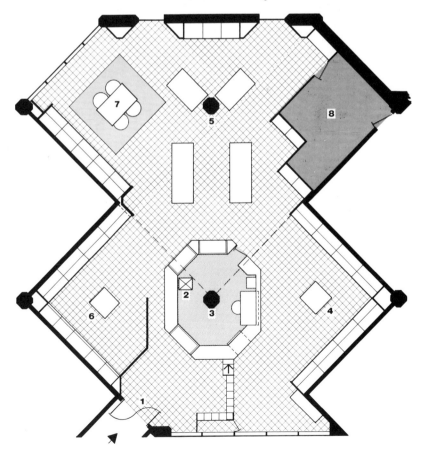

1. Entrance
2. Cashier
3. Floor Office
4. Medical Reference
5. Medical Reference & Textbooks
6. Small Supplies
7. Reference/Browsing Table
8. Receiving/Shipping/Processing

1

2

3

4

5

RIZZOLI INTERNATIONAL BOOKSTORE OF GEORGETOWN, MD

"**H**I," SAID THE MAN at the door. "I'm Fishbait Miller," the retired Senate greeter turned author said. "Come on in." About 30 Washington, D.C., authors and 250 invited guests did just that at Rizzoli International Bookstore and Gallery's champagne reception, celebrating the store's opening in Georgetown's Foundry Shopping Mall.

The entrance doors of the wood-trimmed storefront (1) are flanked by a pair of triangular show windows (2). There, art enthusiasts, members of the diplomatic corps, political figures, university faculties, regular, and casual customers are led to the shop proper through a glassed-in corridor. The surprise is that the glass-lined corridor is actually a gallery for art. Once inside, the 4,000-square-foot bookselling space is divided into three sales rooms by wide arches. The store is serviced from a handsome desk (3) placed in the center of the space.

Lower ceilings, warm tones of ash, plants, and soft incandescent lighting provide the warmth and effectiveness of the background for selling books in this sophisticated shop.

There is a pleasant view from the store out through tall windows to a brick-paved patio, a place for outdoor sales and gatherings. The natural light filtering in pleasantly changes the interior environment of the international foreign language newspaper, magazine, and softbound book sections (4) from hour to hour.

In the center of the store near the service desk is a collection of magnificent art books (5), for which the parent Fifth Avenue store is famous. The enormous stock of foreign language records and books in this Rizzoli store includes the latest bestsellers in Italian, French, Spanish, German, Russian, Finnish, Gaelic, Egyptian, Basque, and Korean (6). Rizzoli's also stocks domestic titles of children's books, cookbooks, travel guides, atlases, dictionaries, art, design, and reference books.

To add to the ambiance, late Baroque background music is periodically played through the store from a fine hi-fi stereo system located in the quality classical record and tape department.

6

1. **Entrance**
2. **Gallery**
3. **Cashier/Service Desk**
4. **Art**
5. **Reference Books**
6. **Foreign Periodicals**
7. **Foreign Language Books**
8. **Classical Records/Tapes**
9. **Children's**
10. **Receiving/Shipping/Processing**
11. **Manager**

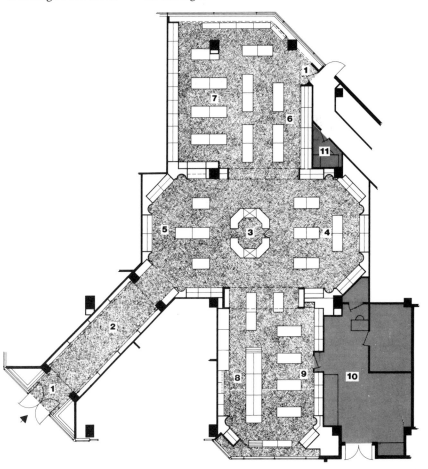

CREDITS

Store	Photographer	Architect
B. DALTON BOOKSELLER, 666 Fifth Avenue, New York, New York	Bill Mitchell	Alfred Nelson, A.I.A.
BARNES & NOBLE SALES ANNEX, Uptown—Radio City, New York, NY	Ken White	—
BARNES & NOBLE SALES ANNEX, Downtown—18th Street, New York, NY	Ken White	—
NEW CANAAN BOOKSHOP, New Canaan, CT	Ken White	—
UCONN CO-OP, University of Connecticut, Storrs, CT	Ken White	Galliher, Schoenhardt & Baier, A.I.A.
BARNES & NOBLE, Westfarms Shopping Mall, Corbins Corner, CT	Ken White	—
THE HARVARD COOP, Harvard Square, Cambridge, MA	Hutchins Photography, Inc. & Harvard Coop	Samuel Glaser Associates
THE TECH COOP OF THE HARVARD COOPERATIVE SOCIETY IN THE MIT STUDENT CENTER, Cambridge, MA	Hutchins Photography, Inc.	Eduardo Catalano, A.I.A.
THE CONTRACT DESIGN CENTER BOOKSHOP, Chicago, IL	Heinrich Blessing	—
RIZZOLI INTERNATIONAL BOOKSTORE OF CHICAGO	Ken White	Fillipo Perego, Milan, Italy
YOUR BOOKSTORE THE INDIANA MEMORIAL UNION, Indiana University, Bloomington, IN	William Turk	—

Store	Photographer	Architect
THE MINNESOTA BOOK CENTER, Minneapolis, MN	Ken White	Meyers & Bennett, A.I.A.
BOOKS UNDERGROUND, University of Minnesota, St. Paul, MN	Ken White	Meyers & Bennett, A.I.A.
GPO U.S. GOVERNMENT BOOKSTORE, Arco Plaza, Los Angeles, CA	Ken White	Alfred Martin, A.I.A.
UNIVERSITY BOOKSTORE, The University of New Mexico, Albuquerque, NM	University Photo Service	Jess Holmes, A.I.A. & Van Dorn Hooker, A.I.A.
GPO U.S. GOVERNMENT BOOKSTORE, Houston, TX	Ken White	—
J. NORTH BOOKSELLER, Fort Worth, TX	Ken White	—
RIZZOLI INTERNATIONAL BOOKSTORE OF ATLANTA, GA	Ken White	Fillipo Perego, Milan, Italy
GEORGIA TECH BOOKSTORE, Georgia Institute of Technology, Atlanta, GA	Bob Geller, Visual Communications	Jova, Daniels & Busby, A.I.A.
UNIVERSITY BOOKSTORE, Virginia Tech, Blacksburg, VA	Virginia Tech Photo Service	Carneal & Johnston, A.I.A. and The Architects Collaborative
DUKE MEDICAL BOOKSTORE, Raleigh, NC	Ken White	Warner, Burns, Toan & Lunde Assoc., A.I.A. and James Ward, A.I.A.
RIZZOLI INTERNATIONAL BOOKSTORE OF GEORGETOWN, MD	Ken White	Fillipo, Perego Milan, Italy, and Vlastimil Koubek, A.IA.

GLOSSARY OF BOOKSTORE PLANNING AND DESIGN TERMS

AISLE: Space devoted to customer and/or materials circulation within a selling area.

AMBIANCE: (Also called atmosphere) The general quality of an interior design representing the store image.

ASSORTMENT: A related collection of books displayed by author or subject. May also refer to the overall stock mix in a department or bookstore, manifesting the variety or selection available.

ASSORTMENT DISPLAY: The technique of presenting one unit of size, style, or color of every selected item of merchandise within a department in a mass display.

BABY BOOKS: Board books, cloth books, and shape books intended for children 2 years old and under.

BACKLIST: All titles other than those published within the current season.

BARGAIN BOOKS: The term used by booksellers to describe (1) books sold at a price lower than the original retail price, and (2) books sold at a comparatively low retail price that never had an original price printed on the jacket.

BARREL VAULT: A roof or ceiling in the form of continuous rounded arches.

BESTSELLERS: Titles identified as the result of the compilation and analysis of sales recorded by selected booksellers throughout the country and ranked by *The New York Times* and *Publishers Weekly* on a weekly basis.

BLOCK PLANS: Design drawings showing divisions of the floor plan into block or area adjacencies. Block plans indicate store entrances, stairways, elevators, department locations, stockrooms, service desks, offices, storage space, and other operational elements in the form of blocks. The store owner can thus preview the alternative department arrangement and customer and service aisle arrangement prior to the fixture layout and detail planning.

BOXED SETS: A group of series, thematic, subject, or individual authored books or merchandise packaged together in cardboard cartons or in a plastic shrink-wrap cocoon.

BUILDER: The individual, partnership, or corporation that contracts for, organizes, and supervises the construction of a building project.

CASH WRAP: The counter in a bookstore where sales transactions, giftwrapping, and occasionally customer service functions take place.

CATEGORY SIGNS: Interchangeable lettered signs, usually made of poster board, indicating the subject matter of display sections in bookstores.

CHECKOUT: A self-selling element designed and located at the exit of an enclosed sales area in a controlled customer traffic pattern. Designed for full-time cashiers and prominently signed.

CIRCULATION PLAN: (Also known as the traffic plan) A plan showing anticipated free customer flow throughout the retail sales areas. Locations of display fixtures, feature displays, sales tables, cashiers and service desks, and other facilities are determined by the circulation plan to assure the best merchandise exposure to the greatest number of shoppers.

CLERESTORY: Windows in the upper part of a wall.

COLOR CONTRASTED: (Also known as "coloring out") A merchandising technique of arranging books or other merchandise by contrasting their colors to highlight the individual graphic quality of each item.

CONTRACT: An agreement, written or verbal, between the bookseller and the store planner, architect, engineer, builder, contractor, individual, or organization agreeing to render service or work. The contract instrument describes the scope of work to be done and designates the responsibilities of each party.

CONTRACTOR: One who is in charge of an entire store construction project, furnishing the material and labor of one or more trades itself, and employing subcontractors to perform all other necessary work. The general contractor, in consultation with the bookseller, store planner, and architect, arranges working schedules and expedites the work to conclusion.

COUNTER: A simple selling fixture used for top display and merchandise storage—generally used for over-the-counter selling by sales personnel.

CURTAIN WALL: A partial overhead wall that "hangs" above the floor on a structural frame. It is sometimes installed above the wallcases in bookstore interiors to give them a custom built-in look.

DANGLER: A promotional sign or device hung overhead from the ceiling.

DECORATING: The planning, composing, and selecting of colors, materials, furniture, furnishings, and accessories to enrich the interior design of a bookstore interior. Used in bookstores to embellish the selling environment and thereby enhance the visual presentation of merchandise.

DEMAND SELLING: The concept of presenting merchandise for "must-have" and planned purchases in which location is not a factor.

DENSITY: The ratio of the net area of selling space to the area occupied by all bookselling fixtures.

DEPARTMENT: A section of a retail bookstore selling and dealing with specialized books.

DESIGN: The art of conceptualizing and sketching, in outline, the interior, plan, architecture, equipment, decorating, graphics, and merchandising of a bookstore.

DETAIL DRAWING: A drawing of any small part of a larger unit showing a particular section of the store design, e.g., table or gondola.

DOMINANCE: The merchandising posture which visually affirms that the bookstore has the most complete inventory and selection of any bookstore in the community which it serves.

DOUBLE DECK STOCK: Floor and mezzanine stockroom space achieved by construction of steel shelving to develop the maximum cubic content of high ceiling space.

DROPPED (OR HUNG) CEILING: A ceiling constructed below the main structure or original ceiling, designed to conceal pipes, HVAC ducts, and obstructions; to provide a plane for the placement of an effective lighting system; and to improve the interior proportions.

DUMP DISPLAYS: A self-display shipping unit made of cardboard supplied to bookstores by publishers and manufacturers. Dumps are primarily intended to feature from 36 to 45 lead title books and special promotions. Dumps are also used for pens, health and beauty aids, soft toys, and other low-priced volume items.

ELEVATION: A scale drawing or design of the front, side, or rear of a bookstore interior or exterior element indicating the design, proportions, and materials of a particular vertical surface. Elevations are made to be "read" in conjunction with a floor plan.

ESTIMATES: Statements prepared by various contractors and suppliers of buy-out items declaring their charges for providing work and materials described on the plans and in the specifications.

ETAGERE: A modular display fixture suitable for bookstore show window and feature display use, consisting of levels of adjustable glass shelving, supported on a polished tubing system.

FACADE: The vertical area or "face" of a store front, or the face or front part of an interior elevation.

FACE OUT: The display of book titles or other merchandise with the full cover or face design of the book visible and facing the customer.

FIXTURE: Any of various selling devices designed to display, present, and store books and merchandise.

FIXTURE DENSITY: The ratio of the area occupied by the store fixtures to the net area of the sales space. The fixture density for bookstores should not exceed 50 percent of the net sales area.

FIXTURES, FLOOR: Any of the cases and display stands used for merchandise presentations and storage. The major types are:
Counters: Enclosed units which are used for merchandising, with a built-up construction added to increase visual presentation.
Gondolas: Center-floor units with adjustable and removable wood, metal, or glass shelves, convertible for the display of hanging or folded merchandise. Gondolas satisfactorily display books and merchandise in a manner that allows the shopper to easily see and touch the items, thus encouraging impulse sales.
Showcases: Cases with glass-enclosed top sections for merchandise display. Occasionally a bottom section is provided for reserve stock. Usually 3 feet 2 inches high, showcases are used for over-the-counter selling of control type merchandise (art supplies, calculators, watches, jewelry, pens, etc.).

FLOOR PLAN: The specific plan layout of a bookstore, including the arrangement of categories, store front, walls, aisles, gondolas, tables, racks, etc.

FUNCTIONAL AREA: Building area including walls, columns, entrances, stairs, escalators, elevators, mechanical equipment rooms, elevator machinery rooms, electrical equipment closets, toilets, pipe spaces, ducts, chases, and permanent hallways not available for retail use.

GALLERY: A raised platform constructed of wood or metal onto which sales departments and supervisory offices are placed.

GONDOLA: See *Fixtures, Floor.*

GONDOLA ENDCAPS: Any of several display stands which accommodate single or multiple assortments of books and merchandise at the end of a gondola, generally on the main aisles.

GOTHIC: An architectural style of the Middle Ages (twelfth to sixteenth century) characterized by the pointed arch.

GRAPHICS: The combination of visual art techniques applied to bookstore design, including typography and lettering, dimensional background effects, mural painting, and signing of merchandise with price, size, and promotional information.

GROSS BUILDING AREA: Total square footage of space occupied by a bookstore building calculated to the outside of the building walls.

HVAC: Heating, ventilating, and air conditioning.

IMPULSE SELLING: The concept of locating merchandise at high-traffic locations in a bookstore to stimulate additional purchases.

ISLAND: An arrangement of cubes, showcases, counters, and back fixtures to create a visual merchandise sales or display unit.

ISP: Institute of Store Planners, the national organization of professional store planners.

JOBBER: A wholesaler merchant who generally specializes in the sale of merchandise to retail bookstores. There are jobbers of virtually every class of consumer goods, including trade hardcover, trade paperback, and mass-market books, stationery, gifts, pens, art material, film, candy, etc.

LOW TICKET: Low priced.

L-SHAPED STEPDOWN: A one-piece unit composed of three steps built in an L shape to fit into or around a corner. Used primarily to feature new arrivals and key titles.

MASS MARKET: A softcover book of standard size for mass distribution through wholesalers and jobbers to various types of booksellers; a book bought at a straight discount where the publisher has paid the freight and the books are cover return.

MATERIALS HANDLING SYSTEM: The equipment and methods of receiving, storing, and moving goods from truck dock to point of sale within the store.

MERCHANDISING: The buying, administering, visual presentation, and selling of books and consumer goods at retail to the public, generally for a profit.

MEZZANINE: (Or Balcony) An area between two floors of a bookstore that is less than half of the floor onto which it is open.

NET SELLING AREA: Is calculated by subtracting the functional area from the gross area. The remaining space is available for selling to customers and includes fixtured sales areas, stockrooms, fitting rooms, cash wraps, and service desks.

NONSELLING AREA: See *Functional Area.*

OPEN PLANNING: A planning and design concept aimed at achieving a total open, flexible, visual sales space by the omission of high walls and partitions.

OVERSIZED TITLES: Books which in physical dimensions are larger than normal, i.e., 10 to 12 inches tall or over.

OVERSTOCK: Duplicate copies of book titles or merchandise which are in excess of the shelf stock to meet immediate demand.

OVERSTOCK AREAS: The shelves above the normal wall display space which are used to display overstock.

PARQUET: Flooring composed of wood blocks or strips of a fixed length.

PILASTER: A rectangular column projecting slightly from a wall and designed to simulate a square column with capital, shaft, and base.

POCKETS: The space assigned to the display of mass-market titles face out in a rack, dump, gondola, or wall section.

PODIUM: See *Gallery.*

PROGRAM BUDGET: An analytical breakdown of costs of time required to complete a proposed project. Budgets vary from "best guesses" to detailed line item estimates.

PROPS: Interesting items, such as plants, furniture, household effects, sporting goods, etc., used to enhance a department or window merchandise display.

PYRAMID PATTERN: Any of a variety of display arrangements of books (arranged face out) or merchandise with most of the bulk (titles) at the base and ascending in a stair-step manner to a single item (title) at the peak on display steps or tables.

QUALITY PAPERBACKS: (Also called trade paperbacks) Paperbacks published by a trade publishing house and sold under a whole copy return.

RAMPS: A gradual sloping floor surface, inclined from one gallery or floor level to another.

REMAINDERS: Publisher's overstocks sold at a new retail price lower than the retail price of the books when first published.

REPRINTS: Books that are reprinted and sold at a lower retail price.

RETURNS: Books or merchandise brought back to the bookstore for credit or exchange by customers.

SALES AREA: The space where sales are transacted, including cashier stations, service and information desks, stockrooms, and fitting rooms.

SALES METHODS: One or more of the following popular methods of selling merchandise may be used in the same bookstore:
Self-Selection: Merchandise is displayed on fixtures to encourage the shopper to touch, examine, and select items without pressure by sales personnel.
Self-Service: Merchandise is displayed on open shelves so that the shopper selects items from the tables, steps, gondolas, or wall units without sales help. Very often, the customer must enter the area through a gate and exit via a checkout counter. Since the shopper is on his or her own, signage is essential.
Over-Counter Selling: Merchandise is shown to the shopper by a salesperson stationed behind a showcase or counter.

SALES VOLUME: The annual gross earnings at retail.

SCALE: All professionally prepared floor plans and elevations are drawn incremental to scales, such as 1/4 inch = 1 foot, in which, for example, the ratio of one-quarter inch on the drawing represents one foot of measurement in the actual project and its objects.

SCHEDULING: A written plan designating the beginning and completion of each step in the work of planning and building a bookstore from inception to the grand opening.

SEASONAL MERCHANDISE: Book or nonbook merchandise, such as calendars, for which sales are concentrated during a particular season of the year.

SECTION: A scale drawing showing a building or object as if cut in two.

SERVICE: All activities supporting the selling function within a bookstore.

SERVICE DESK: (Also known as the information desk) A counter arrangement conveniently located to service the complete store within the sales area, designed to accommodate special order, telephone order, information, and "will call" functions. Decor and signage are important for quick identification.

SHELL: Structural framework of a building, including columns, girders, beams, floor construction, exterior walls, and roof.

SKETCHES: Rough draft drawings made in a freehand technique that outline floor plans, elevations, sections, and perspectives. Sketches are used to explore several possible solutions to a store's specific planning and design problems and to enable the bookseller to visualize and evaluate these solutions.

SPECIFICATIONS: A statement of the scope, details, materials, methods, and performance of a bookstore building project.

STACKER BOXES: Wooden boxes designed to facilitate display build-ups. They are used both as platforms and to provide extra height for the displays.

STEP: A wood display fixture used back-to-back or in conjunction with a display table. Composed of three steps with an overall height of approximately 30 inches and the width of a display table.

STORE PLANNER: An individual with a minimum of 5 years of sound professional experience in his or her chosen specialty, with a strong background in book merchandising, designing, planning, graphics, and a thorough knowledge of bookstore fixtures and features.

STYLE: A particular or distinctive character of bookstore design and decoration associated with contemporary and historic architectural and decorative themes.

TABLE: Any open selling fixture generally designed to contain book and merchandise stock, the horizontal upper surface being used for merchandise presentation.

TERRAZZO: Flooring of chips of marble set in cement and polished.

TITLE DEPTH: The quantity of any particular title on hand or to be ordered.

TRAFFIC: The movement of people or goods through a bookstore, horizontally and/or vertically.

TRANSACTION: The recorded completion of a retail sale.

TRENDS: The recognition of the general direction of book and merchandise buying patterns early enough to take advantage of their sales potential.

TROMPE L'OEIL: An eye deceiver; painted decoration giving a three-dimensional effect.

TURNOVER: A term for evaluating inventory calculated by dividing yearly sales by the average of a 13-month inventory.

UNDERSTOCK: The storage/display space underneath counters and display tables.

VALANCE: A horizontal member located at the top of a wall-height selling fixture, sometimes used for category signage and to conceal a continuous light source.

VENEER: A thin sheet of material (wood, brass, tortoise-shell, etc.) applied to another surface.

VERTICAL COLUMN MERCHANDISING: In wall sections or gondolas, multiple pockets of the same mass-market or trade title displayed one shelf or pocket above another.

WALL FIXTURE: A section of fixtures attached to a perimeter partition for the display presentation and storage of books and merchandise. It may be an integral part of the partition construction or prefabricated, and may have an open or enclosed case.

INDEX